CHILD'S PLAY 6-12

CHILD'S PLAY 6-12

160 Instant Activities, Crafts and Science Projects for Grade Schoolers

Written and Illustrated by

Leslie Hamilton

Crown Publishers, Inc.
New York

Published by Crown Publishers, Inc., 201 East 50 Street, New York, New York 10022. Member of the Crown Publishing Group.

CROWN is a trademark of Crown Publishers, Inc.

Manufactured in the United States of America

Library of Congress Cataloging-in-Publication Data

Hamilton, Leslie, 1950–
     Child's play 6–12 : 160 instant activities, crafts, and science projects
for grade schoolers / written and illustrated by Leslie Hamilton.
        p.   cm.
     Includes index.
     Summary: Presents over 150 crafts, games, and activities,
including things to make out of paper, science projects, recipes,
fabric crafts, and games to play in the car.
     1. Handicraft—Juvenile literature.   2. Science projects—Juvenile
literature.   3. Creative activities and seat work—Juvenile
literature. [1. Handicraft.   2. Games.   3. Amusements.]
I. Title.   II. Title: Child's play six to twelve.
TT160.H333   1992
790.1'922—dc20   91-12883
                                                              CIP

ISBN 0-517-58354-2

10   9   8   7   6   5   4   3   2   1

First Edition

To Larry, Sarah and Dave

"The key to the treasure is the treasure."
JOHN BARTH, *Chimera*

CONTENTS

ACKNOWLEDGMENTS   xv
A NOTE TO PARENTS AND CAREGIVERS   xvi
HOW TO USE THIS BOOK   xvii
BASIC SUPPLIES   xviii

INDOOR PROJECTS AND PAPER CRAFTS   1

● Instant Twin   3
● Pipe Cleaner People/Pencil Riders   4
● 3-D Mural   7
■ Paper Plate Flying Saucer   8
▲ Trolley Rocket   10
■ Cardboard Tube Rocket   14
■ Styrofoam Tray Castle   16
■ Egg-Carton Caterpillar   18
● Racing Spiders   20
■ Egg-Carton Flowers   22
● Walnut Mice   23
● Walnut Boats   24
● Instant Bookcase   25
● Cardboard Box Pet House   26
■ Cereal Box Letter Holder   28
■ Tissue Carnations   30
● Instant Window Garden   32
■ Papier-mâché Mix   34
▲ Papier-mâché Crafts   34

PAPER CRAFTS

- Paper Plane   37
- Paper Plate Plane   39
- Paper Plate Helicopter   40
- Paper Airplane Games   42
- Paper Boat   42
- How to Make a Square Piece of Paper   44
- Paper Basket   44
- Paper Cup   46
- Fortune Teller   48
- Five-Point Stars and Flowers   50
- Drawing Cutouts   52
- Paper Plate Sunburst Hanging   53
- Graphic Bookmark   54
- Lively Lettering   56
- Caption Drawings   58
- Draw Your Own Comic Strip   59
- Make Your Own Note Cards   60
- Stenciling with Paint   61

CLAY PLAY

- Cornstarch Clay #1   63
- Cornstarch Clay #2   64
- Make a Mobile   65
- Tiny Flowers   66
- Toothpick Structures   68
- Dough Heads/Dough Guys   70

SCIENCE FUN   73

- Flutter Wing   75
- Rolling Tubes   76
- Funnel and Candle   77
- Balloon Barometer   78
- Hotter Sunbeams   79
- Möbius Strip   80
- Paper Loops   82
- Pepper/Powder Trick   83
- Changing Colors   84

● Bubble Bouncers — 86
● Penny Cleaner — 87
■ Colder Snow — 88
▲ Test for Starch — 89
▲ Test for Vitamin C — 90
▲ Purple Cabbage Water — 90
▲ Test for Acid and Base — 91

OPTICAL ILLUSIONS
● Optical Spinner — 93
■ Optical Twirler — 94
■ The Illusions — 97
    Tunnels from Spirals — 97
    Circles from Straight Lines — 98
    Color from Black and White — 99
    Color Mixers — 100

SEWING AND FABRIC CRAFTS — **101**

YARN CRAFTS
● Sew-a-Picture — 103
● Yarn Dolls — 104
■ Pom-poms — 106

SEWING CRAFTS
●■ Basic Stitches — 107
■ Tooth Pillow — 108
■ Shape Pillow — 110
■ Sachets — 111
▲ Easy Stuffed Animals — 112
■ Pouch — 115
▲ Mini-Backpack — 118
▲ Belt Pack — 120

CRAYON CRAFTS WITH FABRIC
● Wallhanging — 123
■ Pillow — 124
▲ Pot Holder — 124

BEADING CRAFTS
● Simple Bead Necklace — 126

■ Flower Bead Necklace   127
▲ Indian Bead Necklace   129

WRITING AND THINKING   **131**

● Time Capsule   133
● Make a Scrapbook   134
■ Make a Poster   135
● Start a Collection   136
■ Word Searches with a Theme   140
● ESP Game   141
▲ Make Your Own Board Game   142
■ Codes   144
▲ Maps   145
■ Write to Your Favorite Magazine   148
▲ Write Your Own Newspaper   148
■ Song Writing   150

QUICK AND EASY COSTUMES   **151**

● Gypsy/Fortune Teller   153
▲ Superhero   153
● Rock Star   153
■ Pirate   154
■ Mummy   154
● Hippie   154
▲ Dalmatian   155
■ Flower   156
● Lumberjack/Paul Bunyan   157
● Backwards Boy/Backwards Girl   157
● Politician   158
■ Male Colonist/George Washington   158
■ Female Colonist   158

CARDBOARD BOX COSTUMES
■ Candy Machine   159
■ Dinner Table   161
■ Juice Box   162
■ Television Set   163
■ Gift Box   164

SANDWICH BOARD COSTUMES

■ Tube of Toothpaste   165
■ M & M   166
● Movable Masterpiece   166
■ Board Game   167

ACCESSORIES

● Silver Bead Necklace   168
● How to Make a Mask Stay on Your Head   169
▲ Cape or Apron   170
● Colonial Shoe Buckles   172
■ Quick Knickers   173
■ George Washington Wig   173
● Pirate or Gypsy Earring   174
● Pirate or Gypsy Kerchief   174
● Belt   174
● Gloves   174

OUTDOOR PROJECTS AND ACTIVITIES   175

● Pine Cone Bird Feeder   177
■ Soda Bottle Bird Feeder   178
■ Milk Carton Bird Feeder   180
■ Sponge Prints   182
■ Nature Prints   183
■ Nature Bookmark   185
● Season Placemats   187
● Sidewalk Games   188
● Simple Potpourri   191
● Pocket Bubbler   191
● Helium Balloon Message   192
● Creature Count   193
●■▲ Backyard Exercise Course   194
●■▲ Backyard Scavenger Hunts   196
■ Snow Sculpture   197
● Flashlight Walk   197
● Star Gazing   198

TREASURE HUNTS

- ● Follow the Arrows   199
- ● Follow the String   199
- ● X Marks the Spot   200
- ■▲ Backyard Orienteering Treasure Hunt   201
- ■ Clue to Clue   202
- ■ Clue to Map to Clue to Map   202
- ▲ Neighborhood Hunt   202
- ● Treasure Hunt in the Snow   202

INDEX   203

ACKNOWLEDGMENTS

I am grateful to the following people who contributed ideas, encouragement, or inspiration:

Ana Bolles, Jen Bonaccorsi, Marian Bratcher, David Cohen, Laurie Dolph, Jennifer Galloway, Megan Guy, Alicita Hamilton, Dave Hamilton, Erva Hamilton, Sarah Hamilton, Nancy Henry, Robert Heuchling, Katie Higgins, Aaron Hobson, Ben Hobson, Marc Hubbard, Kenny Kim, Giselle y Diana Medina, Kathy Northrup, Marianne O'Connor, Phil Pearlman, Dana Spang, Jackie Straus, Kim Tansey, and Christine Yost.

Special thanks to Warren Hamilton for his valuable advice on the Science Fun chapter, and to my husband, Larry, who patiently helped me untangle innumerable computer knots.

Extra special thanks to Beryl Anderson and Vivian Pearlman for taking the time to critique the entire manuscript and try so many of the activities with their children.

My editor at Crown, Irene Prokop, has been constantly efficient, supportive, and helpful. A million thank yous.

And finally, to all the school kids who have told me that my crafts, games, and science experiments are "awesome," I think you're pretty awesome yourselves.

A NOTE TO PARENTS AND CAREGIVERS

The time we spend with our children is important and precious. Often, our daily routines and the sometimes hectic schedules of our school-age children leave us few chances to be together. The activities presented in this book will enable you to spend some creative "quality" time with your child, or children, even when that time comes in bits and pieces.

Child's Play 6–12 is a collection of science, outdoor, and crafts projects for children, ages six to twelve. These ideas are all *quick and easy*. You and your child can gather materials and get involved in a project in minutes.

Most of the supplies needed for these crafts and activities are things commonly found in your home (see Basic Supplies, page xviii). Special supplies that you may need to buy are listed separately in a "Plan Ahead" section (see page xviii).

The projects in *Child's Play 6–12* are "open-ended." Your child's interest, ability level, and the time available will determine how simple or detailed the finished product will be. Use the symbol system (see How to Use This Book, page xvii) as a general guide to the time requirements and difficulty level of each activity. Then let your child's curiosity and creativity lead the way.

HOW TO USE THIS BOOK

Each craft or activity in *Child's Play 6–12* is labeled with one or more symbols. Use these symbols as a general guide for the time required and the difficulty level of the project.

● Quick and easy. Requires little, if any, adult help.

■ Medium difficulty. May need some adult help. May take extra time.

▲ Advanced. Requires some adult help to get started. May need adult help or supervision during the activity. May turn into a more time-consuming project if the child gets interested.

Of course, some children may choose to elaborate on a quick and simple ● idea, turning it into an afternoon's activity. Other children may zip through a ▲ craft in a short time, and go on to something else.

Finally, there is a caution symbol: ❗ *Adult supervision is needed for safety.* While the projects and activities in this book are all geared for maximum fun, extra care should be taken during certain science experiments, or wherever the ❗ symbol appears.

BASIC SUPPLIES

The supplies for most of the projects in *Child's Play 6–12* are things commonly found in your home. Certain science experiments and ▲ crafts, however, may require a trip to the store. Some of these items are listed in the "Plan Ahead" section, below.

Basic Supplies: paper, construction paper, scissors, crayons, felt-tipped markers, pencils, ruler, glue, clear tape, masking tape, paints (poster paint, finger paint, or watercolors), balloons, string, rubber bands.

Kitchen and Household Supplies: paper plates, drinking straws, aluminum foil, waxed paper, sponges, paper towels, bleach, iodine, ammonia, pipe cleaners, paper clips, toothpicks, cotton swabs, cotton balls, facial tissues, baking soda, vinegar, salt, sugar, purple cabbage, etc.

Throw-aways You Should Save: egg cartons, cardboard tubes from paper towels and toilet paper rolls, newspapers, colorful magazines or catalogs, used gift wrap, ribbon and fabric scraps, glass juice bottles, Styrofoam grocery trays, cardboard boxes, plastic soda bottles, cardboard milk or juice cartons, cereal boxes, junk mail, etc.

Plan Ahead Items:

Clear Con-Tact paper—self-adhesive paper, sold in rolls or by the yard. Available in hardware and discount stores.

Small glass beads, beading needles, and nylon beading thread—available in craft stores.

Yarn—available at fabric stores and department stores.

Poster board—available in stationery stores, some supermarkets, some drug stores.

INDOOR PROJECTS AND PAPER CRAFTS

● INSTANT TWIN

You need: Set of child's clothes—long-sleeved shirt or sweatshirt, long pants, socks, shoes
Gloves or mittens
Hat
Paper lunch bag
Rubber bands
Safety pins
Markers or crayons
Lots of newspaper

Child does: Chooses clothes to use for Instant Twin. Stuffs crumpled newspaper inside clothing (not shoes or hat). You may want to close sleeve and pant ends with rubber bands.
Draws face on paper bag. Fills bag two-thirds full of crumpled newspaper and twists closed. (This twist forms a "neck.")

You and child do: (See illustration.)
Fit pieces of Instant Twin together by tucking shirt into pants, and by using safety pins when necessary.
Sock tops can go *over* outside of pant legs, and then fit into shoes.
Gloves or mittens fit *over* shirt cuffs.
Stuff neck of paper bag inside shirt collar. Secure with safety pins if necessary.
Fit hat over paper bag head.
Prop in a cozy chair with a good book, or have "twin" join the family for dinner.

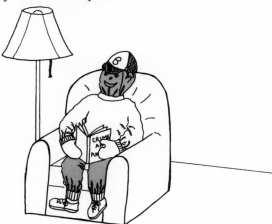

PIPE CLEANER PEOPLE / PENCIL RIDERS
(*Very fast and fun!*)

You need: Pipe cleaners
Paper, scissors, and glue (optional)
Markers (optional)
Toothpicks (optional)
Thread (optional)

You and
child do: (See illustration.)
Each pipe cleaner person requires two pipe cleaners.
Fold pipe cleaner #1 in half. (1)
Form a circle (¼–½ inch across) at the fold, and twist once or twice to form the head and neck. (2)
Fold pipe cleaner #2 so that the ends meet in the middle. (3)
Twist entire pipe cleaner #2 to form the arms. (4)
Insert pipe cleaner #2 under neck of pipe cleaner #1 and twist 3–5 times to form body. The arms should now be tightly secured. (5)

Ideas: Cut out a circle of paper the size of the pipe cleaner head. Glue it to one side of the head. When glue dries, turn figure over and draw face on paper. (6)
Figures can be bent into action stances (ballet pose, gymnastics, karate, running, etc.) (6)
Pipe cleaner people can hold things in loop hands. Try toothpick swords, tiny paper umbrellas, pipe cleaner canes, toothpick ski poles (and cardboard cutout skis), etc.
Make **Pencil Riders** (see illustration.)
This is a nice activity for parties, while waiting for the last guests to arrive. Then children take pipe cleaner figures and pencils home as favors.
Use pipe cleaner people on **3-D Mural,** page 7.
Make a chain of pipe cleaner people holding hands. Form them into a circle and they will stand by themselves.
Pipe cleaner people make great Christmas tree ornaments. Tie a bit of thread or ribbon through top of heads.

PIPE CLEANER #1

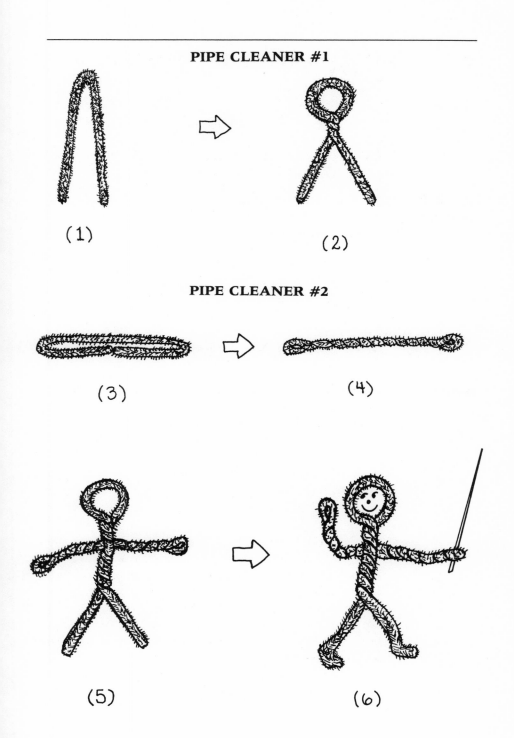

(1)

(2)

PIPE CLEANER #2

(3)

(4)

(5)

(6)

PIPE CLEANER PENCIL RIDER

Note: Pipe cleaners are great for play in the car. Bring a pack of one hundred for long trips and children can make an endless number of things: people, animals, eyeglasses, crowns, jewelry, chains, etc.

3-D MURAL
(This is a nice group activity.)

You need: Large piece of white paper (Freezer paper works well—the bigger the group, the bigger the paper.)

Markers or watercolors (Crayons may be used, but glue doesn't stick as well.)

Cotton balls, pipe cleaners, twigs, construction paper, aluminum foil, toothpicks, magazine pictures, etc.

White glue

Scissors

You and child do: (See illustration.)

Draw or paint a background to cover the entire paper. This may be a very simple line drawing or the children may choose to color in the sky, grass, mountains, add windows to buildings, etc.

Glue three-dimensional objects to mural. (See *Ideas.*)

Ideas: Background is low mountains, blue sky, and green grass. Add cotton balls for clouds, spiral of yellow yarn for sun (or use yellow paper circle). Use pieces of yarn for sun's rays (fray one end, if desired). Cotton balls for sheep; pipe cleaner or toothpick pieces for legs. Toothpick fence. Twigs for trees.

Background is city scene with buildings, streets, and sky. Add cotton ball clouds. Cotton ball smoke from a drawn smokestack. A square or rectangle of clear tape with a paper or marker frame around it looks like a glass window. Department store windows can be filled with pictures cut from clothing catalogs. Populate streets and sidewalks with cutouts of magazine people and cars. Or use **Pipe Cleaner People,** page 4. Yarn or thread for power lines.

Background is child's home in winter time. Add cotton ball clouds, aluminum foil icicles hanging from roof, cotton ball snowman. Pipe Cleaner Person in profile, skiing on Popsicle stick skis.

Background is ocean, sky, and beach. Cotton ball clouds; yellow yarn or paper sun. Spread a thin layer of glue over beach and sprinkle on sand. Glue on tiny pebbles and/or shells. Draw seagulls in flight. Glue on paper sailing ships at sea. (Fabric sails are a nice touch.) Pipe Cleaner Person flying fabric or paper kite on piece of yarn or string. Paper starfish, crabs, pail, shovel, sand castle, etc.

■ PAPER PLATE FLYING SAUCER

You need: 2 paper plates
4 paper cups
Aluminum foil
Tape (clear or masking)
Optional for decoration: pipe cleaners, drinking straws, colored paper, etc.

You and   (See illustration.)
child do: Cover bottom of each plate with aluminum foil, lapping the foil over to the front of the plate. Only the bottoms of the plates will show.

Cover one cup with aluminum foil. Tuck ends of foil inside cup. Secure with clear tape, if necessary.

Cut the tops off the other three cups, so that the remaining cups are about 1½ inches high. (1) Cover these with aluminum foil, tucking the extra foil inside the cups.

(1)

(2)

(3)

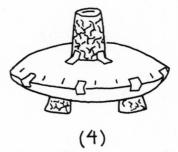

(4)

(5)

Turn large cup upside down and secure to bottom of one plate, using tape. If masking tape is used, *cut* it into 1–2-inch pieces with scissors, so that you get neat-looking edges. (2)

Tape the bottoms of the three smaller cups to the bottom of the remaining plate. (3)

Securely tape the two plates together. (4)

Child does: Decorates with pipe cleaners, straws, paper cutouts, etc. (5)

▲ TROLLEY ROCKET

You need: Stiff paper (a paper plate or an old manila folder works well) cut into a rectangle, 6½ x 5 inches

Or

8-ounce milk carton from school lunch (washed and dried)

Or

4-ounce juice carton from school lunch or snack program (washed and dried)

Ruler

Scissors

Clear tape

1 safety pin (must be 1 inch long)

3 drinking straws

A long piece of thin string (Kite string works well.)

Balloon

You and child do: (See diagram.)

If Using Paper Rectangle

Measure 1½ inches on all sides of paper rectangle, and fold. Open rectangle to reveal fold lines. (1)

Make cuts, as shown. (2)

Fold sides up and secure with tape. (3)

(See **Paper Basket** for hints, page 44)

Tape two drinking straws to the opposite sides inside the paper box. (4)

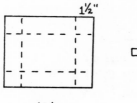

1½"

(1)

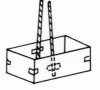

(2)

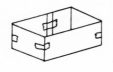

(3)

(4)

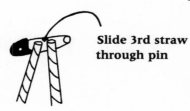

Slide 3rd straw through pin

(5)

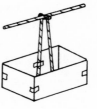

(6)

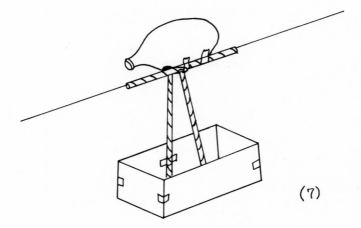

(7)

Pin the tops of the two straws with the safety pin. Slide the third straw through the pin. The fit should be snug. (5 and 6)

Attach one end of the string to a secure spot across the room (doorknob, table leg, etc.) Thread the other end of the string through the third straw.

Blow up balloon. Pinching it closed so air doesn't escape, tape the balloon to the straw, as shown. (7) *Note:* This is most easily done by putting two pieces of tape on the straw and pressing the inflated balloon onto the tape.

Child does: Holds the string taut and releases the balloon. The trolley should shoot across the room on the string.

Variations: (See illustration.)

If Using 4-Ounce Juice Carton
Cut top off carton, as shown in Figure 8.
Follow steps 4–7.

If Using 8-Ounce Milk Carton
Cut windows in sides of milk carton. Tape top closed. (9)
Tape two drinking straws to top, as shown in Figure 10.
Follow steps 5–7.

Ideas: Trolley can be used to transport lightweight items. If two people hold the string taut between them, they can:
- send secret messages back and forth
- trade M & M's
- send over a new balloon
- trade stickers
- trade baseball cards (one at a time)

TROLLEY ROCKET VARIATIONS

Juice carton   **(8)**

Milk carton

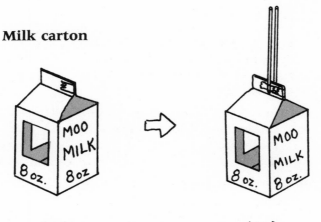

(9)   (10)

CARDBOARD TUBE ROCKET

You need: Cardboard tube from paper towel roll
Two paper plates (or stiff paper)
Ruler
Aluminum foil
Scissors
Clear tape
Markers or crayons

You and
child do: (See diagram.)
Cover cardboard tube with aluminum foil. Secure with tape.
Cut three 3-inch slits in one end of the tube, evenly spacing them around the tube. (1)
Cut three triangles out of the center of the paper plate, as shown. (2) Decorate the triangles, if desired, using crayons or markers.
Insert 3½-inch side of triangles into slits, and secure on both sides with clear tape. Rocket should be able to stand up on its base. (3)
Cut a half circle from the center of the second paper plate, as shown. (4)
Fold half circle into a cone shape and secure with tape. (5) Cut bottom of cone so that it perfectly matches size of cardboard tube. Decorate cone with markers or crayons if desired. Attach nose cone to cardboard tube with clear tape. (6)

Optional: Child can add trim to rocket (NASA labels; windows; smaller, attached rocket on space shuttle made from toilet paper tube).
Attach thread to rocket in two places and hang from ceiling. (6)

14

(1)

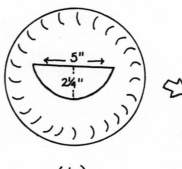

(2)

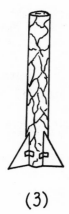

(3)

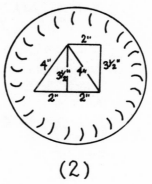

(4)

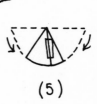

(5)

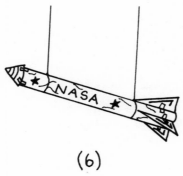

(6)

STYROFOAM TRAY CASTLE
(A fun way to recycle and reuse Styrofoam.)

You need: 2 or more Styrofoam meat or vegetable trays, thoroughly washed and dried
Scissors
Clear tape
1 or 2 drinking straws
Sharp pencil
Fine-tipped permanent marker (optional)

*You and
child do:*   (See diagram.)
Select two Styrofoam trays that are roughly the same size. Cut off the curved edges of one tray. (1)
Cut the tray in half lengthwise. (2)
Cut evenly spaced ½-inch snips along one long edge of each piece. (3)
Snap every other tab off by bending it with your fingers. (Styrofoam breaks easily.) (4)
At the ends of each piece, cut narrow slits as shown in Figure 5, snapping out the thin slice of Styrofoam.
Repeat steps 1–4 for second Styrofoam tray.
Cut narrow slits in the ends of the two new pieces, as shown in Figure 6.
Slide pieces A and B together, as shown in Figure 7.
Fit piece C to the other end of piece A. (8)
Attach piece D to the ends of B and C, as shown. (9)

*To decorate
castle:*   Cut door in castle wall. (10)
Cut drinking straw in half. Cut two triangle shapes from scrap pieces of Styrofoam, and tape to ends of straw pieces, making flags. Tape flags to inside of castle wall on either side of front door. (10)
Use pencil point to poke peep holes in castle walls. (10)
A fine-tipped permanent marker may be used to decorate castle walls with family crest or, for a more realistic look, try drawing *bricks!* (10)

Ideas: Encourage child to create his or her own castle design.
Use trays, tape, and imagination to build towers, high walls, low walls, a drawbridge, ramps, horse corrals, etc.

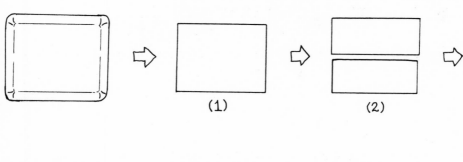

(1)　(2)

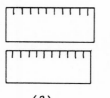

(3)

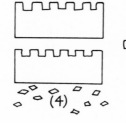

(4)

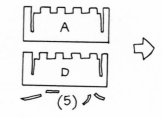

(5)

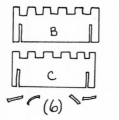

(6)

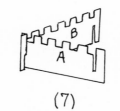

(7)

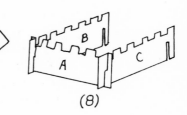

(8)

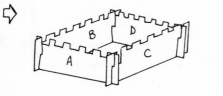

(9)

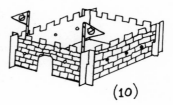

(10)

17

EGG-CARTON CATERPILLAR

You need: Cardboard egg carton
Scissors
Poster paints and brush
Sharp pencil
Yarn and large needle
2 pipe cleaners or toothpicks

You and   (See illustration.)
child do: Cut individual cups from bottom of egg carton. The number of egg cups determines the length of the caterpillar.

Child does: Turns cups upside down and paints outside of individual egg-carton cups.
Paints or draws face on one cup.

You do: When paint is dry, use pencil point or needle to poke two holes in two sides of each cup, as shown. (Do not poke holes through face side of first cup or back side of last cup.)
Thread about 24 inches of yarn on needle. Knot one end of yarn.

Child does: Starting with head, thread yarn through holes to connect egg cups on one side of caterpillar. Leave about 1 inch of yarn between each cup.

You do: End yarn by tying knot on inside of last cup.

Child does: Threads remaining yarn through holes on other side of caterpillar.

You do: End yarn by tying knot on inside of last cup. Poke two holes in top of caterpillar head for toothpick or pipe cleaner antennae.

Note: Egg-Carton Caterpillars can be a fun group project:
- Family Caterpillar—Each family member decorates one or two egg-carton cups. Caterpillar is assembled as family activity. This can be an *ongoing project* as child and other family members paint and attach additional egg cups over a long period of time. Caterpillar grows longer and longer and longer. . . .

- Party Caterpillar—An easy party activity! Each party guest decorates one or two egg-carton cups. Adult assembles caterpillar as souvenir for birthday child.
- Club Mascot—Each club member decorates two or three egg-carton cups at home and brings them to club meeting. Club members assemble caterpillar together.

underside view

● RACING SPIDERS

You need: Egg carton
Scissors
Poster paints or markers
Sharp pencil
4 pipe cleaners
Tape
Marbles (one for each spider)
Tilted surface (a table or coffee table is good)

You and   (See diagram.)
child do: Cut individual cups from bottom of egg carton. (You will
need two cups for each spider.)
Trim the edges of one cup. (1)

Child does: Paints (or colors) outside of egg cup. Draws a face on one
side—scary or happy. (2)

You do: When paint is dry, use pencil point to poke eight holes
around top edge of three sides of egg cup. Do not poke
holes on the face side of the cup. (3)

You and   Push pipe cleaners through holes, in one side and out the
child do: other. Underside of spider should look like Figure 4.
Trim edges of second egg cup so that cup is about a ½ inch
high. (5)
Use a loop of tape to secure the small cup inside the first
egg cup, to cover pipe cleaners.

Child does: Bends pipe cleaner legs into spidery positions. When
racing, legs should be slightly off the table surface. (6)

You and   Make two or more spiders to race. Set each spider over a
child do: marble and place on a tilted surface. Spiders can race
each other to the floor. (6)

Space Blob   (See Figure 7.)
Variation: Use same egg-cup construction as for spiders, but poke
two holes in *top* of egg cup. Weave one pipe cleaner
through holes to form antennae. Decorate face accordingly.

Racing   If pipe cleaners are unavailable or if you're in a hurry,
Snails   simply cut out egg cups, decorate, and set over marbles!
Variation:

Party Idea: Young children might enjoy making and racing spiders, space blobs, or snails at your next party.

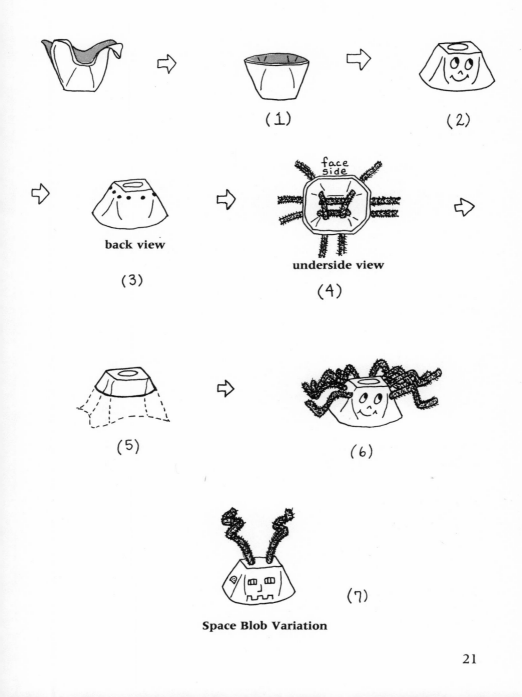

(1)

(2)

back view

(3)

face side

underside view

(4)

(5)

(6)

(7)

Space Blob Variation

21

■ EGG-CARTON FLOWERS

You need: Cardboard egg carton
Scissors
Sharp pencil
Poster paints and brush
Pipe cleaners or toothpicks
Clear tape

You and (See illustration.)
child do: Cut individual cups from bottom of egg carton.
Cut, as shown, to form different flower shapes.
Use pencil point to poke a small hole in the base of flower.
    Push a pipe cleaner or toothpick into the hole, to form
    the stem.
Paint flower, inside and out, using realistic colors or polka
    dots, stripes, and other patterns. (Daisies are especially
    nice with white petals and yellow centers.)
If desired, cut out leaf shapes, paint green, and tape to
    pipe cleaner stem. *Or* form leaf shapes out of a second
    pipe cleaner and attach to stem by twisting in place.

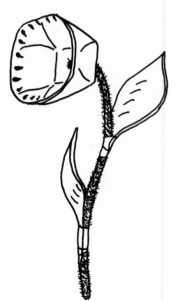

WALNUT MICE

You need: Walnut shells, broken in half
6 inches of string or yarn
Small piece of white paper
Glue
Scissors
Markers

You and   (See illustration.)
child do: Use a marker to draw a pink or red nose on the pointed
end of the shell.
Use black marker to draw eyes, about ½ inch up from the
nose.
Cut ears out of paper, as shown. Color both sides. (Brown
ears with pink centers in front look cute.) Fold ears on
fold line and glue to shell so that paper tab is *behind*
ears. (When glue dries, gently bend ears over a pencil,
to curve them forward.)
Cut string in half. Tie a knot in the middle of one piece of
string. Fray the ends. Glue the knot over (or a little
below) the nose.
Tie a knot in one end of the second piece of the string.
Glue the knotted end inside the shell, for a tail. Fray the
other end of the string.

Idea: Try putting a marble inside the shell and have "Mouse
Races" on a tilted surface.

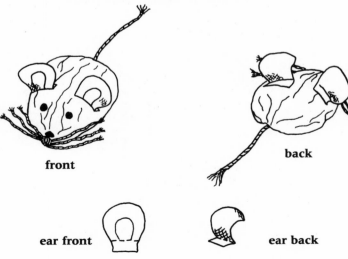

front

back

ear front   **ear back**

WALNUT BOATS

You need: Walnut shells, broken in half
Cornstarch clay (Recipes, pages 63 and 64.)
Toothpicks
Paper
Scissors

Child does: Places marble-size ball of clay inside walnut shell half.
Inserts toothpick into clay for mast.

You do: Dry walnut boat(s) in microwave on High for about 1
! minute.

You and (See illustration.)
child do: Cut sails out of paper, and thread onto toothpick mast.
Experiment with different sail designs.
Test seaworthiness in sink, basin, bathtub, or wading
pool.

● INSTANT BOOKCASE

You need: Cardboard box
Ruler
Pencil
Sharp knife or heavy scissors
Poster paints, markers, construction paper, gift wrap, prepasted wallpaper scraps, or Con-Tact paper

You and
child do: (See diagram.)
Turn box bottom up. Use ruler to measure and draw cutting lines, as shown in Figure 1.

You do: Use knife or heavy scissors to cut along cutting lines. If desired, trim the bottom of the bookcase back a few inches. (2)

Child does: Decorates *outside* of bookcase with poster paints, markers, construction paper, Con-Tact paper. Scraps of prepasted wallpaper work especially well. (3)

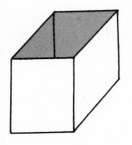 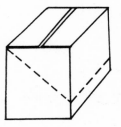

(1)

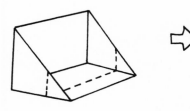 

(2)   (3)

CARDBOARD BOX PET HOUSE

(A quick house for a favorite stuffed animal or doll.)

You need: 2 cardboard boxes roughly the same size
Ruler
Pencil
Sharp knife or heavy scissors
Poster paints, markers
Construction paper
Scissors
Tape

You and child do: (See diagram.)
If boxes are slightly different sizes, determine which is smaller in length. Set this smaller box aside. It will be the living area of the house. Turn larger box over. Use ruler to measure and draw cutting lines, as shown in Figure 1. Roof should be equal measurements on both sides.

! *You do:* Cut along cutting lines to form the roof. (2)

You and child do: Construction paper shingles add a nice finishing touch. Cut 2×4-inch rectangles and tape overlapping rows to roof, starting at bottom. (3)

Child does: Draws cutting lines on second box for door and windows.

! *You do:* Cut along child's cutting lines. (4)

Child does: Leaves house as is, or decorates outside with paints, markers, or construction paper. (5)

Ideas:
- Make a number of different size pet houses and create a village.
- Make a high-rise pet apartment building. Cut windows and doors in 2 to 4 similar-size boxes. Stack them, secure with strong tape, and top with a roof. Child may want to write each occupants' name above the door.

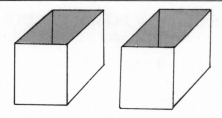

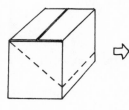 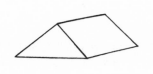 

(1) (2) (3)

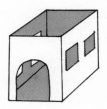 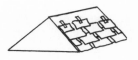

(4) (5)

CEREAL BOX LETTER HOLDER

(This makes a nice gift!)

You need: Empty cereal box (6½–7 inches across is the best size)
Scissors
Ruler
Pencil
Clear tape or glue
Decorative paper—construction paper, homemade paper, recycled gift wrap, color comics, fabric, etc.

You and child do: (See diagram.)
Cut top flaps off box.
Measure 6 inches up from bottom of box on both sides and back. Draw cutting lines. (1)
Measure 3 inches up from bottom of box on both sides and back. Draw folding lines. (2)
Leaving front of box intact, cut down all four corners of box, to fold lines.(3)
Leaving front of box intact, cut sides and back of box on cutting lines. (4)
Fold back of box on folding line and tuck inside box. Fold sides on folding lines and tuck inside box. (5)
Fold top edge of box front down. Tuck inside box so that top edge touches box bottom. (6)
Secure with tape or glue.
Cover surfaces with decorative paper or fabric.
Using pencil point, carefully punch hole in tall side of box, as shown. (7) Letter holder can be hung or used on a desk.

SOGGO
FIBER
FLAKES

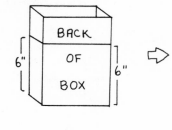

BACK
OF
BOX

6"   6"

(1)

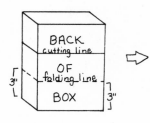

BACK
cutting line
OF
folding line
BOX

3"   3"

(2)

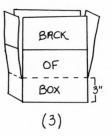

BACK
OF
BOX

3"

(3)

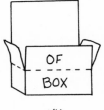

OF
BOX

(4)

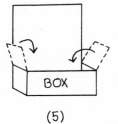

BOX

(5)

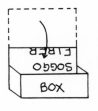

SOGGO
FIBER
BOX

(6)

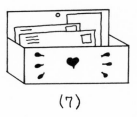

(7)

29

■ TISSUE CARNATIONS

You need: Two-ply facial tissues (any color)
Thread (color should be matching or close to tissues)
Scissors
Pipe cleaners (optional)
Felt-tipped markers (optional)

You and
child do:

(See diagram.)
Open one facial tissue out flat. (1)
Fold in half the long way. (2)
Make a series of pleats about ½–¾ inch wide, back and forth, for length of tissue. (3 and 4)
Wrap thread tightly around middle of tissue about five or six times, and tie securely. (5)
Trim edges off both ends of tissue. (6)
Carefully separate all four layers of tissue, on both sides of thread. (7)
Gently gather puffy tissue in one direction, with tied center on the bottom. (8)
Attach pipe cleaner stem and paper leaves with tape, if desired. (8)
For added color, highlight edges of tissue with marker.

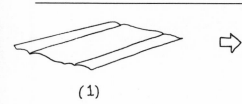

(1)

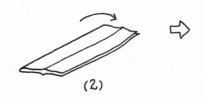

(2)

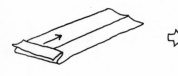

(3)

(4)

(5)

(6)

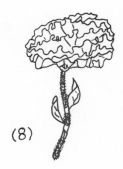

(7)

(8)

INSTANT WINDOW GARDEN

(This activity comes from a family from Alaska, where winters are very dark and very long.)

You need: Clear Con-Tact paper
                Colorful construction paper
                Scissors

You and   Cut out and create a collection of beautiful and colorful
child do: paper flowers, complete with stems and leaves. You
                may want to add paper grass, a paper butterfly or
                honeybee, and a bright paper sun. (See illustration.)

                Decide how large or small your window garden will be
                and cut a piece of Con-Tact paper accordingly. If
                desired, you can decorate an entire window.

                Carefully peel the backing off the Con-Tact paper. Lay the
                Con-Tact paper sticky side up on a flat surface.

                Arrange your paper garden on the sticky side. Be sure to
                leave some Con-Tact paper exposed in the center of the
                garden and along all four sides.

                Stick the flower garden directly to the window and
                pretend it's summer!

Ideas: Other window decorations might include paper cutouts of
                rainbows, palm trees, tropical fish, jungle animals,
                people, jet planes, rocket ships, robots, planets, and
                moons, etc. Simply cut out construction paper figures
                and assemble as described above.

Note: Removal of window garden is simple. Con-Tact paper
                peels right off.

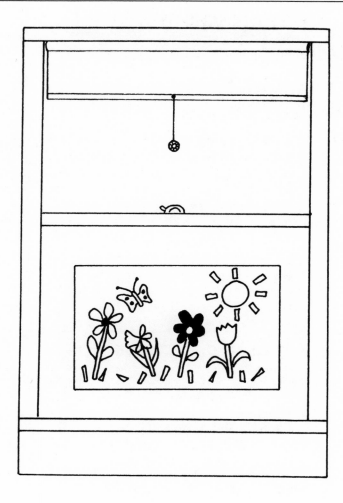

■ PAPIER-MÂCHÉ MIX

You need: White flour
Water
Medium-size bowl
Cup measure
Mixing spoon

You and
child do: Boil 1 cup of water.
In separate bowl, mix ¼ cup flour and ¼ cup cold water
until smooth.

You do: Remove boiling water from heat and quickly stir it into
flour mixture.

You and
child do: Stir mixture until smooth.
While mixture cools, prepare materials for **Papier-**
Mâché Crafts (see below).

▲ PAPIER-MÂCHÉ CRAFTS
(Finished sculpture in 1 hour or less!)

You need: Papier-mâché mix (See recipe above.)
Old newspapers
1–2 white paper towels
Materials for "form": crumpled newspaper, egg-carton
cups, cardboard tubes from toilet paper, masking tape,
toothpicks, etc.
Waxed paper
Poster paints and brush

You and
child do: Cover work surface to protect against drips.
Use loosely crumpled newspaper or other materials to
make a form for your sculpture. You may want to tape
pieces of form together with masking tape. (1)
Tear newspaper into lots of thin strips, about 1 inch wide
and 4–8 inches long.
Dip one strip of newspaper into bowl of mix. Run the
paper strip through your fingers to get rid of excess mix,
and apply to form. Repeat, over and over again, until
form is covered with at least 3 or 4 layers of wet
newspaper strips. (2)

34

When figure is completely covered and smooth, add a layer of white paper towel strips, lightly dampened with papier-mâché mix. This will make the dry figure easier to paint. (If figure is very soggy, you may not need to dampen paper towel strips with mix).

Drying instructions:

!

Microwave—Under constant adult supervision, dry sculpture in microwave. Set it on waxed paper and microwave on High for 1 minute at a time, turning sculpture over after each minute. Depending on size and sogginess of sculpture, drying should take anywhere from 5 to 15 minutes.

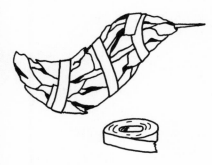

(1)

(2)

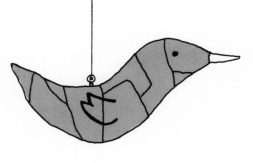

(3)

WATCH CAREFULLY near end of drying time to prevent scorching. Dry figure will be fairly hard and ready for painting.

Or

Air-Drying—Set sculpture in a dry place and allow to air-dry. Depending on sunshine, humidity, and how soggy the figure is, air drying can take anywhere from a few hours to a few days.

Child does: When sculpture is completely dry and hard, child can paint it with poster paints.

You and child do:

!

Painted sculpture can be air-dried or dried in microwave on waxed paper. Microwave on High for 30–45 seconds on each side, removing sculpture when paint loses its wet look.

You and child do: For a shiny finish, cover painted figure with clear polyurethane. Allow to *air-dry.*

A small eye hook can be screwed into figure for hanging, if desired. (3)

Papier-mâché tips:
- Have an idea of what to make *before* you start.
- Always work around a form.
- Think *small*. Especially for your first attempt, it's best to make something small—about 4–6 inches long.
- Try not to let your figure get too soggy. Remember to run the newspaper strips between your fingers to get rid of excess mix.
- Always have an adult present during microwave drying.

PAPER CRAFTS

● **PAPER PLANE**

You need: Rectangular paper, 8½ × 11 inches
Ruler
Pencil
Tape
Crayons or markers
Paper clip (optional)

You and   (See diagram, page 38.)
child do: Fold paper in half, the long way. Unfold paper to reveal fold line down the center.

Measure 3¾ inches up from the bottom of the paper on both sides. Mark these points with a pencil. (1)

Fold top corners in along line between center and pencil marks. The second corner will overlap the first corner. (2) and (3)

Turn paper over. Measure 2 inches from point and fold point down. (4)

Fold plane in half along center fold line, so that point is *inside*. (5)

Measure 1 inch up from center fold and fold each side down. (6)

Note: Plane is very flyable at this point, if you wish to stop here.

You and
child do: Measure 1 inch from edge of paper and fold each edge up. (7)

Tape plane sides together along top. (8)

Note: You may want to weight nose of plane with paper clip.

Child does: Decorates and flies plane.

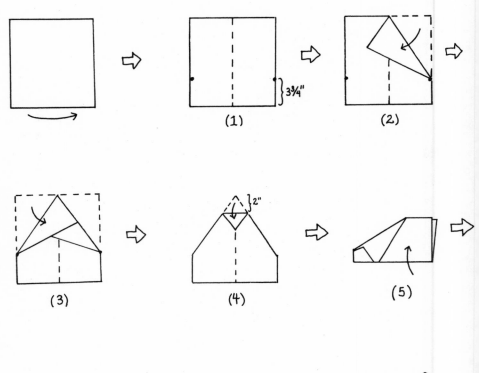

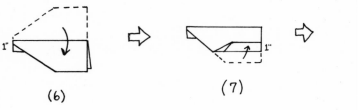
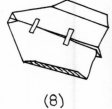

PAPER PLATE PLANE

You need: 2 lightweight paper plates
2 drinking straws
Ruler
Pencil
Scissors
Clear tape
Paper clip
Crayons or markers

You and
child do: (See diagram, page 40.)

From the center of one paper plate, measure, draw, and cut out a triangle with a 5-inch base and 7-inch sides. (1)

Fold triangle in half the long way. (2)

Measure ¾ inch from fold, as shown, and fold sides down along folding line. (2) and (3)

Cut straws so that you have one 4-inch piece and one 5-inch piece.

Securely tape the 4-inch straw into the nose of the plane, so that 2 inches extend beyond the point, as shown. Insert a paper clip in the end of the straw. (4)

Securely tape the 5-inch straw into the back of the plane, down the center fold, so that 2 inches extend out the back, as shown. (5)

From the center of the second paper plate, measure, draw, and cut out a circle about 3 inches in diameter. Cut the circle in half.

Set aside one half circle. Cut a ½-inch slit in the center of the *straight* edge of the other half circle, as shown. (6)

Cut a ¾-inch horizontal slit in the end of the drinking straw and insert the half circle, forming tail. Secure with tape on top surface only. (7)

Cut the remaining half circle in half. Cut a thin slit along one straight edge, *as shown.* The resulting tab should be thin enough to slide into the drinking straw. (8)

Slide tab into drinking straw and secure vertical tailpiece with tape, top and bottom. (9)

Child does: Decorates and flies plane.

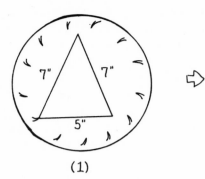
(1)

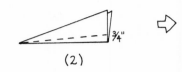
(2)

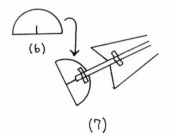
(3)

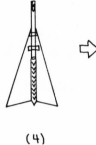
(4)

(5)

(6)

(7)

(8)

(9)

● PAPER PLATE HELICOPTER

You need: Lightweight paper plate
Drinking straw
Ruler
Pencils
Scissors
Clear tape
Crayons or markers

40

You and
child do: (See diagram.)

Cut out shape from paper plate, as shown, with 2-inch base, 3½-inch sides and 3½-inch top. (1)

Cut down center of shape, stopping 1 inch from bottom edge. (2)

Cut 1-inch slit through one end of drinking straw.

Insert bottom edge of paper into slit in straw, as shown. (3) Secure with tape.

Bend one wing forward and one wing back. Gently bend edges of wings, so that they both curve slightly down. (4)

Child does: Decorates helicopter.

Stands on chair and drops helicopter. (Helicopter flies straw downward, as shown in Figure 4.)

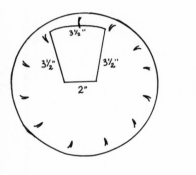

(1)

(2)

(3)

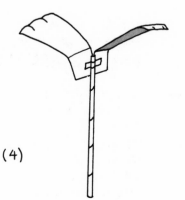

(4)

41

PAPER AIRPLANE GAMES

(Can be played alone or with a group.)

Safe Landing

(This is harder than it sounds.) Try to throw a plane so that it lands inside a *large* laundry basket, pot, or hoop set on the floor. Start close and then move farther away with each successful landing. If you don't have a good landing area, use a towel or any well-defined target as your landing spot.

Loop-the-Hoop

One person holds a hoop (Hula-Hoop, large embroidery hoop, inflated lightweight innertube) as the other person tries to sail a plane through the hole.

Farthest Flight

Standing in the same place for each flight, fly planes for distance. Fly the same plane to find its record flight, or compare different style planes to find the best flier.

Longest Hang Time

Use a stopwatch to time the planes for longest time in the air. Helicopters are good for this!

Most Beautifully Decorated

Not a game, but a fun and creative activity.

PAPER BOAT

(This paper boat really floats!)

You need: Rectangular paper

You and   (See diagram.)
child do: Fold paper in half the short way. (1)
Fold paper in half in other direction. (2)
Unfold Step 2 to reveal fold line. (3)
With folded edge on top, fold corners down to meet at fold line. (4)
Fold bottom flaps up on both sides. (5)

Pull out from point **X** on each side and flatten, tucking in
   end flaps. (6)
Fold bottom corners up on both sides. (7)
Grasp center of each side at **X,** pull out, and flatten. (8)
Grasp **A** and **B,** pull sideways, and flatten. (9)
Fill out center of boat. (10)

Child does: Decorates with crayons, if desired, and floats boat in
   water.

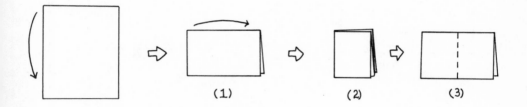

(1)   (2)   (3)

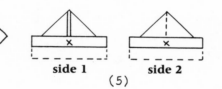

side 1   side 2
(4)   (5)

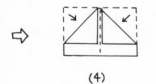

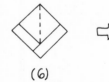   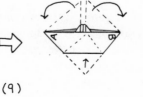   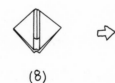

(6)   (7)   (8)

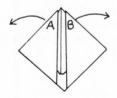   

(9)   (10)

HOW TO MAKE A SQUARE PIECE OF PAPER

Here is an easy way to turn a rectangular piece of paper into a square without using a ruler. (See diagram.) Bring corner **A** down to the bottom edge, and crease the diagonal. Cut from **A** to **B** and open paper up, revealing a perfect square.

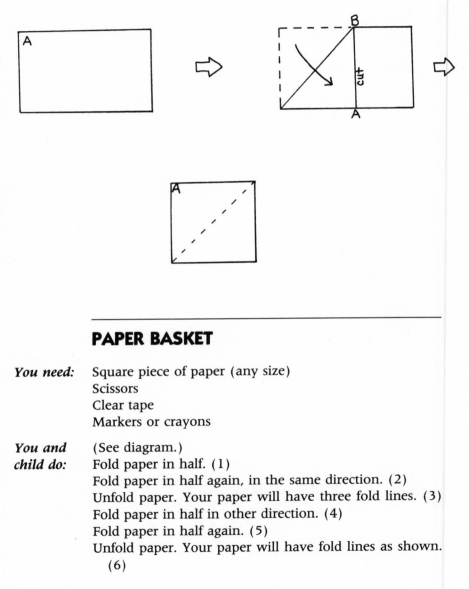

PAPER BASKET

You need: Square piece of paper (any size)
Scissors
Clear tape
Markers or crayons

You and child do: (See diagram.)
Fold paper in half. (1)
Fold paper in half again, in the same direction. (2)
Unfold paper. Your paper will have three fold lines. (3)
Fold paper in half in other direction. (4)
Fold paper in half again. (5)
Unfold paper. Your paper will have fold lines as shown. (6)

Cut along fold lines as shown in diagram. (7)
Bring the edges of tabs A and B together and tape.
Bring edges of tabs C and D together and tape. (8)
Fold outer flaps up and secure with tape. (9)
Paper handle may be added, if desired. (10)

Child does: Decorates basket with markers or crayons.

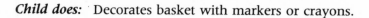

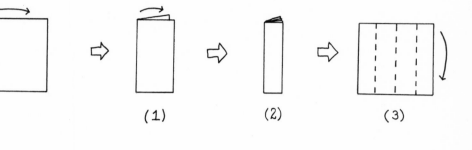

(1)   (2)   (3)

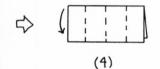 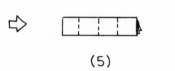 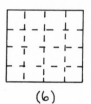

(4)   (5)   (6)

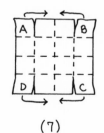 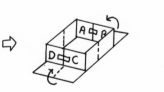

(7)   (8)   (9)

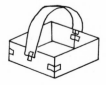

(10)

PAPER CUP

You need: 8½ x 8½-inch piece of paper (Notebook paper, plain white paper, or junk mail are fine. Newspaper or construction paper absorb too much water and don't work!)
Ruler
Pencil

You do: (See diagram.)
Label the 8½ x 8½-inch piece of paper *exactly* as shown in Figure 1.
Measure *exactly* 3½ inches from corner A along the top of the paper. Put an **X** at that spot. Measure 3½ inches down from corner **A**, along the edge of the paper. Put an **O** at that spot. (2)

You and child do: Turn paper over so writing is face down.
Fold paper in half so that A meets C. Then turn paper so that A and C are at the top and B is on the right. (3)
Fold so corner B touches **O**. (4)
Fold so corner D touches **X**. (5)
Fold corner A down. (6)
Turn cup over and fold corner C down. (7)
Open up the top to form a cup. You can drink out of it! (8)

Note: Once your child has mastered the above technique, he or she can experiment with different size paper.

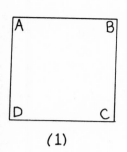

(1)

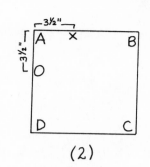

(2)

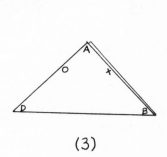

(3)

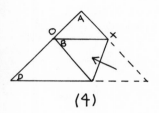

(4)

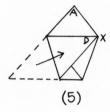

(5)

(6)

(7)

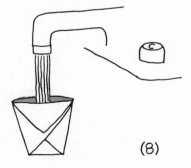

(8)

FORTUNE TELLER

(Kids sometimes call these "cootie catchers.")

You need:　Square piece of paper
Pencil or pen
Crayons or markers

You and　(See diagram.)
child do:　Fold paper in half. (1)
Fold paper in half in other direction. (2)
Open paper to reveal fold lines. (3)
Fold corners toward center. (4)
Turn paper over and fold corners toward center again. (5)
Number this side of paper as shown. (6)
Lift each numbered flap and write a fortune. (7)
Turn paper over and color the four quarters of the paper as shown. (8)
Fold paper in half, so that colored sides are on the outside. (9)
Pinch edges **A** and **B** and push toward each other. (10)

Child does:　Opens the four colored paper flaps out and inserts the index finger and thumb of both hands in the spaces created under the colored flaps. (11)
The fortune teller opens and closes in two directions.
A "fortune" is told by asking a player to:
1. Choose a color—Fortune teller then opens and closes as the color is spelled. (e.g., Red would result in opening and closing three times. Green would be five times, etc.)
2. Choose a number—Fortune teller then opens and closes as number is counted. (e.g., Six would result in opening and closing six times.)
3. Choose a number again—Repeat previous step with a different number.
4. Choose a number again—Fortune teller is laid flat and chosen numbered flap is lifted to reveal "fortune."

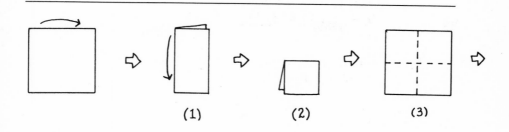

(1)　　　　　　(2)　　　　　　(3)

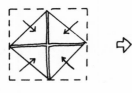

(4)

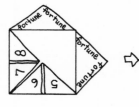
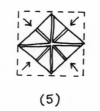

(5)　　　　　　(6)

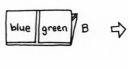

(7)　　　　　　(8)　　　　　　(9)

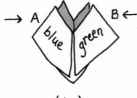

(10)

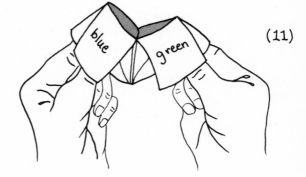

(11)

49

■ FIVE-POINT STARS AND FLOWERS

You need: Piece of paper, approximately 8½ × 11 inches
Scissors
Ruler
Crayons or markers (optional)

You and (See diagram.)
child do: Fold paper in half the short way and label corners, as shown. (1)
Find the halfway point between corners A and D, and label that spot **E**. (2)
Fold paper so that corner C touches halfway mark **E**. (3)
Label point **F**, as shown in diagram. (4)
Fold right edge of paper over to meet line **EF**. (5)
Fold corner D over to meet right edge. (6)

To make a Cut as shown in Figure 7.
star:

To make a Cut as shown in Figure 8.
flower:

For an open Cut along big fold, as shown in Figure 9.
effect:

Child does: Colors stars or flowers.
Mounts on construction paper backing.
Hangs in window, on walls, etc.

Note: This is a good way to get a pattern for an evenly-shaped star. (Comes in handy for school "flag projects.")
Adult can iron stars or flowers flat, if desired.

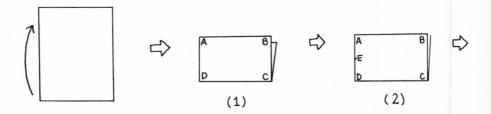

(1)   (2)

50

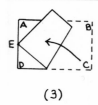  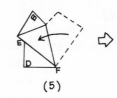

(3) (4) (5)

  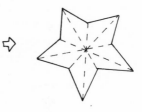

(6) (7)

(8)

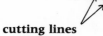 

cutting lines

(9)

cutting lines

51

● DRAWING CUTOUTS

You need: Paper
Markers or crayons
Scissors

Child does: (See example.)
Draws a simple picture that includes figures to be partially cut out (e.g., house, tree, car, person).
Cuts out figures, leaving bottom of drawing *uncut*.
Bends figures up to create three-dimensional effect.

Ideas: Use ideas of perspective by drawing large figures at bottom of paper, and smaller figures closer to the top of the paper. When cut out and bent up, the large cutout will look "close up" and the small cutout will appear to be far away.
Reserve the top 1½ to 2 inches of the paper for distant background (e.g., sunset, mountains, horizon, cityscape, etc.). When this piece of the drawing is bent up, it acts as background or scenery for the three-dimensional scene.

PAPER PLATE SUNBURST HANGING

You need: 2 lightweight paper plates
Ruler
Markers, crayons, or paints
Scissors
Tape
Needle and thread (for hanging)

You and   Draw a circle about 3 inches in diameter in the center of
child do: one plate.
Mark off every 2 inches along the outside edge of the same
plate. There should be *fourteen* evenly spaced marks. (1)
Put the two plates together and cut from each mark down
toward the circle, cutting through both plates. (2)
Cut every *other* wedge out of the circle. (3)

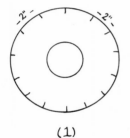

(1)

(2)

(3)

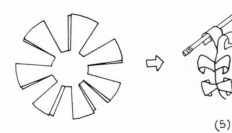

(4)

(5)

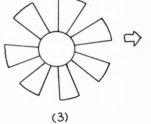

(6)

Child does: Decorates both sunburst shapes with markers, crayons, or paint, leaving center of plate bottoms blank.

Using loops of tape on the center of the plate bottoms, tapes sunburst shapes together on inside, matching "rays" as much as possible. (They won't match perfectly). (4)

Curl rays of sun outward by rolling each ray gently around a marker or pencil. (5)

You and child do: Use needle to poke a small hole near edge of inner circle. (6)

Hang in window.

UFO Variation: Decorate plates with UFO motif (black crayon or marker, bits of aluminum foil, etc.) Omit step 6, and throw UFO horizontally, like a Frisbee.

■ GRAPHIC BOOKMARK

You need: Graph paper
Construction paper
Colored pencils or fine-tipped markers
Scissors
Glue

You and child do: (See examples.)
Working from *center* out, plan a geometric design based on squares of graph paper. The design should be within a rectangle about 5–6 inches long and 1–2 inches wide.

Note: Symmetrical designs work well. Or try diagonal stripes, random colors, etc. A border is also a nice touch. (See examples.)

You and child do: For younger child, adult may want to put a dot of color in desired squares. Child then fills in squares, using color dots as guide.
An older child can do this unassisted.

Child does: Cuts out finished design.
Glues design to construction paper. (Choose a color that complements design.)

Cuts out bookmark, leaving a ¼–½-inch construction
paper border around graphic design.

Ideas: If bookmark is a gift, write something nice on the blank
side:

- a short poem
- "I love you," "I like you," "To a special friend," etc.
- Person's name in **Lively Lettering** (see page 56).

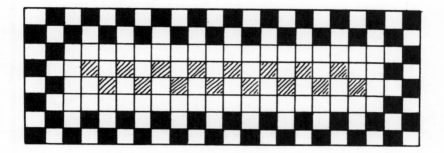

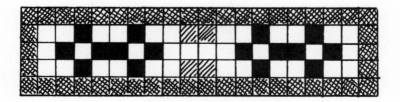

■ LIVELY LETTERING

You need: Paper
            Pencils, pens, or markers

Child does: Experiments with different lettering to write name, short
            messages, notes, posters, etc. 3-D, Bubble, and Theme
            Lettering may be colored in.

3-D Lettering

ABCDEFGHIJKLMNOP
QRSTUVWXYZ

Dot Lettering

ABCDEFGHIJKLMNOPQR
STUVWXYZ

Bubble Lettering

ABCDEFGHIJKLMNOPQRSTU
VWXYZ

Fancy Lettering

$$\mathcal{ABCDEFGH}\,ijk\,\mathcal{l}\,m\,n\,o\,p$$

$$\mathcal{QRSTU}\,v\,w\,x\,y\,z$$

Theme Lettering

CAPTION DRAWINGS

You need: Paper
             Pencils, markers, and/or crayons

Child does: Thinks up funny or imaginative caption for drawing, and
                writes it on top or bottom of page. (See *Ideas.*)
                Draws picture based on caption.

Ideas: "When dragon kids come home from the first day of
           school." (See example.)
           "My family, if we each weighed 500 pounds."
           "Santa Claus takes a surfing vacation."
           "My teacher as a little kid."
           "Outer-space aliens at the grocery store."
           "My family if we were only 2 inches tall."
           "Recess in the year 2050."
           "How I'll look when I'm old."
           "What superheroes do on their vacations."
           "A flying saucer looking for a parking space at the mall."
           "How I look from a bug's point of view."

■ DRAW YOUR OWN COMIC STRIP

You need: Plain white paper
Pencils
Ruler
Markers
Stapler or needle and heavy thread (optional)

Child does: Decides on theme of comic strip (e.g., family adventures, superhero, animal adventures, comic strip characters, etc.).

You and child do: (See example.) Divide page into evenly spaced panels for drawings.

Child does: Draws comic strips in pencil, coloring them in later, if desired. (This can be an ongoing project.)

Ideas: "Adventures of Super Bug," "The Secret Life of Me," "The Wizard of Ooze," "Chirpy Meets the Mugwumps," etc.

You and child do: If desired, you can bind a collection of strips into a comic book, using either staples or needle and thread. Don't forget a colorful cover!

■ MAKE YOUR OWN NOTE CARDS

You need: Plain white paper
Markers, crayons, pens
Scissors
Tape or glue
Clear Con-Tact paper
1 or more of the following:
Gift wrap with pictures on it (floral, juvenile, holiday, etc.)
Old magazines
Color comics
Photographs
Pressed, dried flowers
Paints
Stencils (page 61)
Markers, crayons

You and child do: Cut white paper into note card size: 6 × 7 inches, folded, will fit into a standard envelope. Or make cards slightly larger and make your own envelopes. Fold paper in half and put note card decoration on front page. Cover decoration with clear Con-Tact paper.

Ideas: Choose favorite character from color comics and cut out figure. Attach figure to note card with small amount of glue or tape. Child thinks up an original saying to write on card, inside comic strip "balloon." (See Example 2.)

Cut out figures or attractive and colorful designs from gift wrap, magazines, or unwanted photographs. Attach to note card with small amount of glue or tape. Write message, if desired.

Make a simple stencil (see **Stenciling with Paint,** page 61) and stencil the front of note cards. (It is not necessary to cover stenciling with Con-Tact paper.)

Try simple block printing with poster paints (e.g., potato prints, thumb prints, pieces of sponge dipped in paint, etc.) Or try **Nature Prints,** page 183, and **Sponge Prints,** page 182. It is not necessary to cover printing with Con-Tact paper.

Draw a simple (or fancy) picture, or draw your own cartoon character.

Cut small stars or flowers (pages 50 to 52) out of construction paper or gift wrap. Mount on note card and cover with clear Con-Tact paper.

Cut clear Con-Tact paper to correct size for note card. Remove backing, sprinkle *small* amount of glitter on sticky side, and carefully attach to front of card.

(1)

(2)

▲   **STENCILING WITH PAINT**

You need: White paper
Pencil
Glossy paper (Magazine or catalog covers work beautifully; or try glossy magazine or catalog pages, junk mail, glossy coupon pages, waxed paper, freezer paper, etc.)
Scissors
Clear tape
Poster paints
Clean kitchen sponge
Something to protect work surface

Child does: Decides on and roughly sketches stencil design on scrap paper.

You and child do: Make stencil by folding and cutting small shapes out of glossy paper.

For a single stencil, simply fold the paper once and cut out a half-shape. (1)

For a repeating line of stencils, fold paper in half, in half again, and then in half a third time, all in the same direction. Cut out half-shape from side with large fold. (2)

Experiment with different folding and cutting techniques to get the patterns and designs desired.

You do: Cut a piece of sponge that measures approximately 1½ inches long and ½–1 inch wide. (You may want to cut a number of these.)

You and child do: Position stencil on white paper and hold or tape in place. (Older children may not need to tape stencil.)

Child does: Dips end of sponge piece in *small* amount of poster paint. Lightly dabs paint over area to be stenciled.

Experiments with textures of sponge stenciling by using more or less paint, dabbing softly versus hard, using blotting motion as opposed to painting strokes, etc.

Carefully lifts stencil from white paper.

Note: Rinse sponge pieces with water, to be used again.

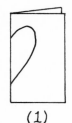 

(1)

 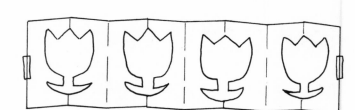

(2)

CLAY PLAY

Cornstarch clay is a fast and easy modeling material suitable for fun or school projects. While larger, three-dimensional sculptures (bowls, creatures, amorphous blobs, etc.) do best when air-dried, you can dry thinner creations in a microwave or conventional oven. (See drying instructions for Mobile, page 65.)

Both recipes can be doubled easily.

CORNSTARCH CLAY #1
(This clay is especially easy to roll very thin.)

You need: Small pot
Metal spoon
Plate
½ cup cornstarch
1 cup baking soda
¾ cup plus 2 tablespoons water

You and child do:

!

Combine all ingredients in pot. Stir constantly over medium-high heat. Mixture will foam and then thicken as it comes to a boil.

When mixture is consistency of mashed potatoes and pulls away from bottom of pot, remove from heat.

Dump dough onto plate and allow to cool, covered with a wet paper towel.

When cool, knead dough on counter or tabletop dusted with cornstarch, until smooth. If clay is too sticky, add a little more cornstarch and knead.

Note: Food coloring can be added during cooking or kneading.
Makes 1½ cups clay.
Store in plastic bag in refrigerator. If clay becomes sticky,
roll in a dusting of cornstarch and knead slightly.
Can be painted when dry.

■ **CORNSTARCH CLAY #2**

You need: Small pot
Metal spoon
Medium-size bowl
½ cup cornstarch
1 cup salt
⅔ cup cold water
Paper towel

You and Put salt and ⅓ cup water in pot. Bring to a boil over
child do: medium-high heat and stir.

!

Dump cornstarch into bowl. Add remaining ⅓ cup water
and mix well.
Carefully add cornstarch mixture to salt mixture. Stir over
medium-high heat. Mixture will thicken rapidly and
pull away from sides of pot.
When clay gathers as lump on spoon, remove from heat.
Dump out on table and let cool, covered with a damp
paper towel.
Dust tabletop or counter with cornstarch and knead until
smooth.

Note: Food coloring can be added during cooking or kneading.
Makes 1½ cups clay.
Store in plastic bag in refrigerator. If clay becomes sticky,
roll in a dusting of cornstarch and knead lightly.
Can be painted when dry.

▲   **MAKE A MOBILE**

You need: Cornstarch Clay, pages 63–64 (Cornstarch Clay #1 is easiest to roll thin.)
Rolling pin
Cookie cutters
Drinking straw
Poster paints and brush
Yarn or heavy thread
Paper towels (microwave safe, if using microwave)
Attractive stick, chopstick, coat hanger, dowel, etc.

You and   (See illustration.)
child do: Work with small amounts of modeling material. Start with a lump about the size of a walnut.
Roll dough or clay as thin as possible (about ⅛ inch) on flat surface. You may want to dust the surface lightly with cornstarch.
Transfer rolled-out clay to paper towel. Cut out shapes with cookie cutters, removing excess scraps of clay.
Use drinking straw to poke a hole in top of shape.

Drying   *Microwave*—With two paper towels *beneath* shapes and
instructions   two paper towels *covering* shapes, microwave on Medium for 1 minute. Check shapes for hardness. Continue to cook on Medium for 30 seconds at a time, checking for hardness after each interval. Shapes will puff slightly.

!

Or

Conventional Oven—Transfer shapes to nonstick cookie sheet. Bake in 200–250° F oven for 10 to 15 minutes. Check shapes often to avoid overcooking. (Less puffing occurs when shapes are dried in conventional oven.)

Or

Allow to *air-dry* overnight on paper towel.

Child does: Paints dry shapes.

Note: If painting causes shapes to soften, simply microwave on Medium for 15 seconds at a time, checking for hardness.

Child does: Cuts yarn into 12-inch lengths. Threads and ties lengths of yarn to shapes.

You and
child do: Attach shapes to stick, chopstick, dowel, coat hanger, etc., so that mobile is balanced.
Or
These shapes may be used as holiday ornaments when tied with short loops of yarn or ribbon.

▲   **TINY FLOWERS**

You need: Cornstarch Clay #1, page 63.
Toothpicks
Waxed paper
Food coloring (optional)
Paints and paintbrush (optional)

You and   (See illustration.)
child do: Separate clay into golf ball–size lumps. Knead one or two drops of food coloring into lumps of clay until you get the colors you want.
Roll clay into about 6 pea-size balls. Flatten the first ball between sheets of waxed paper until it is very thin. (1)
Roll first thin circle of clay around end of toothpick. (2)
Add thin circles of clay, one at a time, layering them around the toothpick end until you have the flower you want. (3)
Gently bend edges of petals outward.

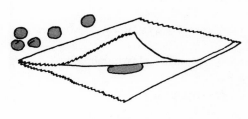

(1)

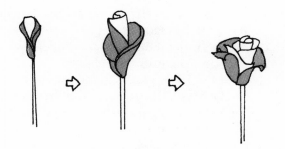

(2)

(3)

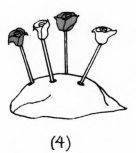

(4)

Note: Tiny flowers can be dried in the microwave (1 minute on High), but they will puff slightly. The petals will stay thin and delicate if *air-dried*. Use a lump of clay as a base to hold toothpick stems. (4)

■ TOOTHPICK STRUCTURES

You need: Either Cornstarch Clay (see recipes pages 63–64)
Toothpicks (LOTS!)
A base to build on—cardboard, plastic placemat, paper plate, etc.
Poster paints and brush (optional)

Child does: Rolls clay into about 20 pea- or marble-size balls.
Uses clay or dough balls to connect toothpicks to form two- and three-dimensional shapes. (See illustrations.)

Note: Build structures *on* base, so they can be moved without damage.

Ideas: Two-dimensional shapes—triangle, square, rectangle, pentagon, hexagon, etc. (1)
Common three-dimensional shapes—pyramids, cube, geodesic structures (see Figures 2, 3, 4, and 5).
Ask child to build Figure 2 and Figure 4. Which is easier to build? Which is sturdier? Children can learn firsthand that three-dimensional structures need support; that geodesic structures are stronger.
Or let child's imagination take over! (6)
When dough hardens, toothpick structures may be painted, if desired.

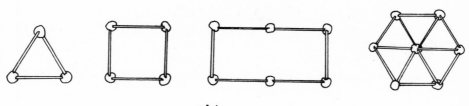

(1)

(2)

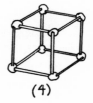

(3)

(4)

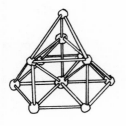

(5)

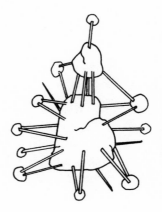

(6)

▲ DOUGH HEADS/DOUGH GUYS
(These funny heads harden in 2 minutes in the microwave!)

You need: Cornstarch Clay #1 or #2, pages 63 and 64.
Dull pencil
Waxed paper
Poster paints and brush
Optional trim (fine-tipped markers, toothpicks, spaghetti, angel hair pasta, curly pasta, elbow macaroni, etc.)

You and child do: (See illustration.)
Roll clay into a smooth walnut-size (or smaller) ball. Use pencil point to poke eyes, nose, and mouth in one side of ball. Poke *deeply*, ¼–½ inch.
Gently flatten bottom of ball so that head stands upright.
Gently squeeze features to alter expression. (Pushed-down forehead results in squinty eyes. Sideways squeeze results in surprised look.)

Ideas: Roll tiny balls of clay and attach as eyes or nose.
If a long, pointy nose is the look you want, form that feature *first,* and then poke eyes and mouth with pencil.
Attach tiny clay balls squeezed thin to make mouse ears.
Trim with pasta or toothpick pieces. Short pieces of toothpick or spaghetti can make spiked haircut. Spaghetti or angel hair pasta makes good whiskers. Curly noodles look like hair. Elbow macaroni can be oversized ears. Toothpick piece with ball of clay at the end can be a pipe.

You and child do:

!

Set finished Dough Head on waxed paper and place in microwave. Microwave (High) for 1½ to 2 minutes, until *hard.* Some puffing will occur.
Head will be hot but cools quickly.
Check for hardness. If head is still soft, microwave for 15 to 30 seconds more.
Let cool as you make more Dough Heads.

Child does: Leaves Dough Heads plain, or paints with poster paints. Small details can be added with fine-tipped markers.

Dough Guys (See illustration.)
Variation: Follow the same procedure as for Dough Heads, keeping figures walnut-size or smaller. Add feet, arms, bulbous

eyes and nose, pointed heads, etc. Use a toothpick to add fine details. Paint with poster paints.

Dough Guys and Dough Heads often have so much built-in character that they are easy to name. Your child may want to paint them, name them, and start a collection.

DOUGH GUYS

SCIENCE FUN

FLUTTER WING

You need: Strip of paper 1 × 6 inches
Drinking straw
Clear tape

You and   (See illustration.)
child do: Tape straw to paper, as shown, overlapping 1 inch of
straw onto paper.

Child does: Blows *hard* into straw. Paper should rise and flutter as
blast of air travels over it.
(If paper doesn't rise, try again with a harder blow.)

What's   The faster air moves, the lower its pressure (Bernoulli's
going on?   principle). The fast-moving air *above* the paper has a
lower pressure than the still air *below* the paper. The
higher pressure below the paper pushes the paper up.
This also shows how airplanes fly. Airplane wings are
built in such a way that the air *above* the wing travels
faster than the air beneath the wing. The air pressure is
greater beneath the wings and this keeps the plane
aloft.

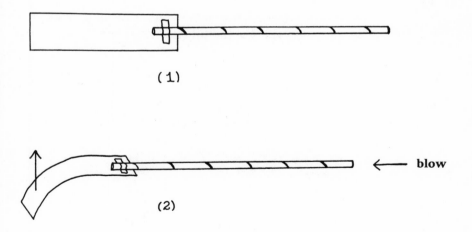

(1)

(2)   ← blow

■ ROLLING TUBES

You need: 2 squares of paper, about 5 × 5 inches
Clear tape
2 long pencils
Drinking straw

You and   (See Figure 1.)
child do: Roll squares of paper into two tubes and tape along edge.
Make sure seam is smooth.
Lay pencils on flat surface about 3 inches apart and tape
down.
Place paper tubes across pencils, about 1 inch apart.

Child does: (See illustration.)
Positions straw between tubes from the side, as
shown. (2)
Blows hard into straw. Tubes will roll together.
Replaces tubes as in Figure 1, and blows between tubes
from above. (3) Tubes will roll together.

Note: If tubes don't roll together, try blowing *harder* directly
between them.

What's   The faster air moves, the lower its pressure (Bernoulli's
going on?   principle). The strong blast of air from the straw, as it
travels between the tubes, has less pressure than the air
on the outer sides of the tubes. The higher air pressure
pushes the tubes together.

blow   (1)   blow

(2)   (3)

● FUNNEL AND CANDLE

You need: Candle and matches
              Funnel

! *You do:* Light candle.

Child does: Blows a *gentle* puff of air to blow out candle.

You do: Relight candle.

Child does: (See illustration.)
              Holds funnel as pictured in Figure 1.
              Puts mouth to small opening of funnel and *uses same gentle puff,* trying to extinguish candle. (It should be difficult to blow out candle.)
              Turns funnel around (Figure 2) and uses same gentle puff to extinguish candle.

What's going on? The air in Figure 1 expands into the broad end of the funnel and is dispersed. Not enough air gets to the flame to blow it out. When the funnel is turned around, the air is concentrated in a strong, narrow stream and easily extinguishes the flame.

blow →

blow →

(1)   (2)

BALLOON BAROMETER

You need: Empty small-necked glass bottle (10-ounce size or smaller is best.)
Balloon
Hot tap water in a bowl
Cold tap water in a bowl

You and child do: (See illustration.)
Fit balloon over top of bottle. Fit must be very tight. (1)
Place bottle in bowl of *very* hot tap water. Be careful!
Wait a minute and watch the balloon. (2)
Place bottle in bowl of cold water. What does the balloon do now? (3)

What's going on?   The hot water heats the air inside the bottle. The air molecules move faster, causing an increase in air pressure inside the bottle. This fills the balloon.
When the bottle is placed in the cold water, the air is cooled and the air molecules slow down. The air pressure drops and the balloon deflates.

Other things to try: Try putting your Balloon Barometer in a sunny window. Can the sunshine warm the air enough to inflate the balloon? If you put the barometer in a bowl of ice cubes, does the balloon deflate faster?

(1)

(2)

(3)

78

▲ HOTTER SUNBEAMS

You need: Large piece of cardboard (14 × 14 inches or larger)
Magnifying glass (1–2-inch size is best)
Outdoor thermometer
Scissors
Table
Pencil and paper
A sunny window

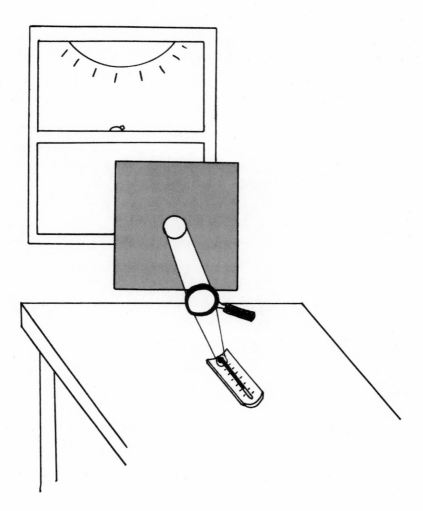

You and
child do: (See illustration, page 79.)
Cut hole the size of magnifying glass in center of card-board.

Move table near window, in bright sunshine.

Hold cardboard in front of window, as shown, so that beam of sunlight coming through hole falls on table.

Position thermometer so that the bulb is in spot of light on table. Wait one minute and record the temperature.

Hold magnifying glass in front of beam of light coming through the hole in the cardboard, as shown. A smaller sunbeam will result. Move thermometer bulb into this sunbeam. Within a *few seconds*, thermometer will register rising temperature.

!   BE CAREFUL NOT TO DAMAGE THE THERMOMETER OR TABLE SURFACE WITH THIS HOT SPOT!

What's
going on? Sunlight heats the area it strikes. The magnifying glass concentrates all the sunlight coming through the hole into a smaller area, which therefore gets hotter.

This same idea explains why it is hotter when the sun is directly overhead at noon, and cooler in the morning and evening, when the sunlight arrives at an angle and is more "spread out."

 ## MÖBIUS STRIP

(This is a way to write on both sides of a piece of paper, without lifting your pencil or turning the paper over!)

You need: Paper (8½ × 11 inches is a good size)
Scissors
Tape
Pencil or marker

Child does: Cuts strip of paper 11 inches long and about 1½ inches wide.

Writes **A** on one end of strip and **B** on other end. (1)

You and
child do: (See illustration.)
Turn strip over so that letters are face down with **B** on the left and **A** on the right. (2)

Bring the two ends together to form a loop. (3)
Turn the **B** end over so that the **A** and **B** are touching. (4)
Secure with tape. The twisted loop that is formed is now
a one-sided surface called a "Möbius strip."

Child does: Starting at any point on the Möbius strip, child draws a
line down the center of the paper and continues
drawing until the circle is complete. (5) Without lifting
the pencil, child will draw a line on both sides of the
paper.

Other
things to
try: Cut Möbius strip down the center line. A larger loop with
a double twist is the result. What happens when you
cut *that* loop down the center?

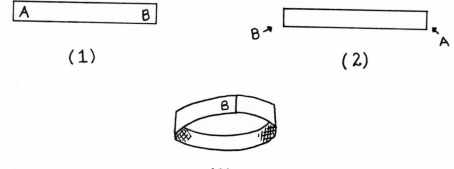

(1)   (2)

(3)

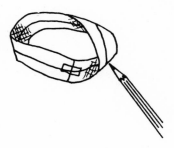

● PAPER LOOPS

You need: Paper (8½ × 11 inches is a good size)
Scissors
Tape

Child does: Cuts strip of paper 11 inches long and about 1½ inches wide.
Writes **A** on one end of strip and **B** on other end. (1)

You and (See illustration.)
child do: Turn strip over so that letters are face down with **B** on the left and **A** on the right. (2)
Bring the two ends together to form a loop. (3)
Turn the **B** end over so that the **A** and **B** are touching, as in the Möbius strip. Then turn the **B** end over *again,* so that the **B** is facing up again. (4)
Secure with tape.

Child does: Cuts down center of twisted loop.
Two *connected* twisted loops will result. Child can continue cutting loops down the center to get a series of very twisted, interconnected loops.

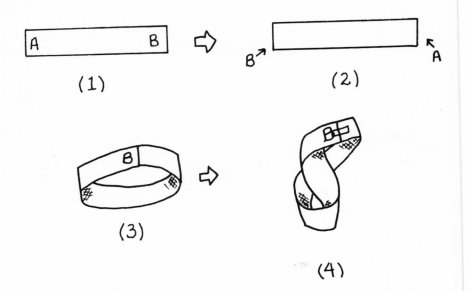

PEPPER/POWDER TRICK

You need: Cereal/soup bowl
Toothpicks
Black pepper
Talcum powder
Liquid dish detergent
Shampoo
Water

You and
child do: (See illustration, page 84.)
Fill bowl with water and let stand until water becomes still.

Sprinkle pepper on the water so that it evenly covers the surface. Note how most of the pepper floats on top of the water. (1)

Dip a dry toothpick into the center of the water. Nothing happens.

Coat the end of a dry toothpick with a drop of shampoo and dip into center of bowl, holding it there for two or three seconds. The pepper will rush to the sides of the bowl. (2)

Rinse out bowl and refill with water. Let stand until water is still and then sprinkle evenly with talcum powder.

Coat end of dry toothpick with shampoo and dip into center of bowl, holding it there for a second or two. The floating film of powder will break up into pieces. (3)

Coat the end of a dry toothpick with liquid dish detergent and dip it into the center of the bowl, holding it there for two or three seconds. The powder will move toward the edges of the bowl and start to sink.

What's
going on?   Plain water has more surface tension than soapy water. When shampoo or detergent are dipped into the center of the bowl, surface tension there weakens. The stronger tension near the edges of the bowl pulls the water surface, carrying the pepper or powder outward.

Dish detergent is a wetting agent. That means that it permits water to penetrate the surface of the powder, causing it to sink.

Other	Encourage your child to experiment to see how other
things to	substances affect surface tension. Try a wet bar of soap,
try:	a drop of cooking oil, a drop of rubbing alcohol, etc.

(1)   (2)

(3)

▲   CHANGING COLORS

! *Note of* *caution:*	This activity uses bleach. Adult supervision is necessary at all times.
You need:	Short, clear glass or jar (approximately 8-ounce size)
	Teaspoon for stirring
	Measuring spoon
	Measuring cups
	Food coloring
	Household bleach
	Water
	White paper

You and ❗ *child do:*	Protect work surface and clothing from possible contact with bleach or food coloring.		
You do:	Explain dangers of bleach to child. Only *adult* should pour bleach during this experiment.		
Child does:	Measures ½ cup water into glass or jar. Adds *one* drop green food coloring to water. Stirs solution.		
You do:	Add ¼ teaspoon bleach to green water.		
Child does:	Stirs solution and observes the surprising result!		
You and child do:	This is a great opportunity to really experiment! Encourage your child to try different color, water, and bleach combinations. You may want to record your findings on paper, like this:		

Water	Color	Bleach	Result
½ c	1 drop green	¼ t	blue
½ c	1 drop yellow	¼ t	clear
½ c	1 drop blue	¼ t	?
½ c	1 drop red	¼ t	?
½ c	1 drop red 1 drop green	¼ t	?
½ c	1 drop red 1 drop blue	1 t	?

Note: Some color changes may take a few minutes to occur. Be patient! Certain solutions will change from one color to clear to a *second* color over time.

Use a piece of plain white paper as a background so you can more easily note subtle color changes.

BUBBLE BOUNCERS

You need: Clear carbonated soda: soda pop, seltzer, club soda. The soda must be fresh, not flat!

Or

Make a mixture of 1 cup water, 5 teaspoons vinegar, and 2 teaspoons baking soda.

5 small raisins (or large raisins cut in half)—Pick fresh, moist raisins. Dry ones don't work as well.

Optional: a few small buttons, unpopped popcorn, salted peanuts

Clear drinking glass or jar

Teaspoon

Baking soda

Salt

You do: Fill the glass three-quarters full of carbonated soda.

Drop in five raisins or raisin pieces. Wait for a minute and watch as the raisins float to the surface and then sink to the bottom of the glass. They will do this over and over again.

Drop in a few buttons, peanuts, or popcorn. Watch what they do.

Sprinkle a pinch of baking soda into the glass. Watch what happens.

Dump about half a teaspoon of baking soda into the glass and stir. What happens now?

Sprinkle some salt into the glass. Watch what happens. Leave the glass alone for 5 minutes. Are the raisins still moving? How about 15 minutes later?

What's going on?   Soda pop is a pressurized solution of carbon dioxide gas and water. The carbon dioxide comes out of the water in the form of bubbles. Opening a bottle or can of soda releases the pressure and lets the carbon dioxide escape slowly.

When you drop the raisins into the soda, bubbles of carbon dioxide gas cling to their bumpy surfaces. When enough bubbles are clinging to a raisin, it rises to the top of the glass. There, the bubbles pop and the raisin drops down again.

Any solid that is added to the soda in the glass (dry beans,

86

a pebble, salt, baking soda, sugar, etc.) forces more carbon dioxide gas to be released. That's what all those bubbles are. If the solid is just the right weight, it will rise and fall in the soda.

● PENNY CLEANER

You need: Salt
Vinegar
Teaspoon
¼ cup measure
Small bowl
Tarnished (dark) pennies
Paper towel
Toothpick (optional)

You and child do: Pour 1 *heaping* teaspoon of salt in bowl.
Add ¼ cup vinegar.
Stir until salt dissolves.

Child does: Drops dirty penny into solution. After about 10–20 seconds, the penny is clean!

Other things to try: "Half and half"—Submerge penny only half way in solution until submerged half is clean. Blot dry with paper towel.
"Polka-dot penny"—Dip end of toothpick in solution and dot surface of dirty penny with tiny drops. When the drops turn light, blot penny with paper towel.
"Keep Abe Clean"—Dip end of toothpick in solution and carefully clean Abe Lincoln's profile. Blot dry. Or carefully clean the background, leaving Abe dark.

What's going on? Vinegar is a weak acid called acetic acid. Adding salt changes the vinegar to a stronger acid called hydrochloric acid. The hydrochloric acid combines with the tarnish on the pennies to form copper chloride, which dissolves away.
Lemon juice contains another weak acid (citric acid) that works in much the same way, changing to hydrochloric acid when combined with salt.

COLDER SNOW

You need: Fluffy snow (or *very* finely crushed ice)
Medium mixing bowl
Salt
Measuring cup
Spoon
Outdoor thermometer

You and   (See illustration.)
child do: Collect 3 to 4 cups of snow in bowl.
Insert thermometer in snow. You may want to pack the snow around the thermometer bulb to get a more accurate reading.
Wait 5–10 minutes and record temperature. Unless it is *well* below freezing outside, the temperature of the snow should be at or close to 32° F (the freezing point of water).
Remove thermometer.
Add ¼ cup salt to snow and mix well.
Replace thermometer in salty snow and watch as temperature rapidly falls. Wait 3–5 minutes to find lowest temperature. Wait 15 minutes and note temperature again.
Experiment with greater amounts of salt (½–1 cup). See how low you can get the temperature to go.

What's going on?	The rapid drop in temperature when you added salt to the snow demonstrates two scientific principles. First, salt lowers the temperature at which water freezes. When you mix salt with the snow, the snow starts to melt.
	Second, the rapid temperature drop during the early melting is caused by a physical phenomenon called the "latent heat of melting." Melting actually causes the snow to *lose* heat.
	Eventually, the temperature rises again as the mixture is warmed by the air in the room.

▲ **TEST FOR STARCH**

You need:	Tincture of iodine (Available in drug stores.)
	Water
	Small jar with tight-fitting lid
	Teaspoon
	Measuring cup
	Test items: white flour, cornstarch, salt, sugar, baking soda, bread, paper, laundry starch, etc.
You and child do:	Pour ¼ cup water into jar.
	Add about five drops iodine to water and shake. Water will be a light brown color.
	Add about ½ teaspoon flour to the jar and shake. Solution will turn purple.
	Make up new solution of iodine and water and experiment with different substances. Anything with starch in it will cause the solution to turn purple or black. If no color change occurs, or solution remains light brown, no starch is present.
	Drop some of the solution on a piece of potato or bread and watch what happens.

TEST FOR VITAMIN C

You need: Tincture of iodine
Water
Cornstarch
Measuring cup
Measuring spoons
Clear glass jar with lid
Teaspoon
Test items: lemon juice, orange juice, milk, soda, water, etc.

You and child do: Pour ½ cup water in jar.
Add ½ teaspoon cornstarch and stir to dissolve.
Add ⅛ teaspoon iodine to solution and stir. Solution will turn purplish black. This liquid is your test solution for vitamin C (ascorbic acid).
Pour 3 teaspoons lemon juice into jar lid.
Add 1 teaspoon of purple test solution to lemon juice.
Stir. Solution will lose its dark color, indicating presence of vitamin C.
Rinse jar lid and experiment with other test items, mixing them with the purple solution. If the mixture loses its dark color, vitamin C is present.

PURPLE CABBAGE WATER

(This solution tests for acid or base.)

You need: Purple cabbage
1 cup measure
Hot water
Food processor or blender
Strainer
Jar with lid

You do: Fit food processor with steel blade.

Child does: Fills 1 cup measure with small pieces of purple cabbage leaves. Dark outer leaves are best.
Dumps cabbage into food processor or blender.

You and
child do:
!

Add 1 cup of very hot water to cabbage pieces. Process or blend for about 30 seconds, until a purple mush is formed.

Let mixture stand for about 10 minutes. While you wait, you and your child can prepare supplies needed to **Test for Acid and Base,** below.

After 10 minutes or so, strain the mush, saving the purple water. Discard mush.

Purple cabbage water can be stored in your refrigerator in a tightly closed jar for 2–3 days.

▲   ## TEST FOR ACID AND BASE

You need:

Purple cabbage water, page 90
White paper plate
Pencil or ballpoint pen
Teaspoons (or an eyedropper)
Cookie sheet or aluminum foil (to protect work surface)
Substances for testing: tap water, ammonia, white vinegar, baking soda, bar of soap, lemon juice, orange juice

Child does:

Lists substances on paper plate, as shown (see illustration). Be sure to leave room between testing areas.
Places paper plate on cookie sheet or aluminum foil.

You and
child do:

Work in the kitchen, near the sink. Using tip of teaspoon (or eyedropper), place a drop or two of purple cabbage water in circle labeled "Nothing." Wait a minute or two and observe color change.

[*Note:* The purple cabbage water reacts with the paper plate and turns blue. Different types of white paper will react differently and produce varying shades of blue.]

Place a drop or two of cabbage water in the circle labeled "Vinegar." *Using a clean teaspoon,* add a drop or two of white vinegar to the drops of cabbage water. The solution will turn pink.

Place a drop or two of cabbage water in circle labeled "Ammonia." Add one or two drops of ammonia. The solution turns green.

!

Repeat procedure for each of the test substances. Be sure to use a clean teaspoon each time, to avoid contami-

nating any solutions. When testing soap, simply rub a
bar of soap on the drops of cabbage water.

**What's
going on?**

The cabbage water is an indicator of acid or base. It turns
pink-to-red when in the presence of acid (vinegar,
lemon juice, orange juice). It turns greenish when
exposed to a base (ammonia, soap, baking soda).

**Other
things to
try:**

Child can think up and test many other substances
(antacid tablet, clear soda pop, milk, pickle juice, etc.).
Child can make homemade indicator paper by cutting
notebook paper in thin strips. Dip the strips in cabbage
water, lay them out on aluminum foil, and let them dry.
Store the dry strips in a tightly sealed plastic bag. Test
liquids by dipping the strips in the liquids and observing
the color change.

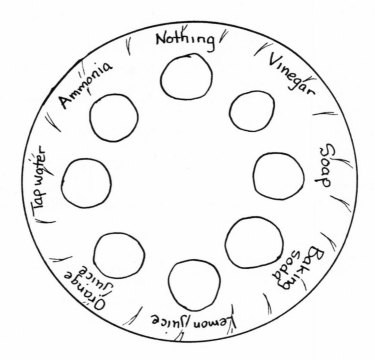

OPTICAL ILLUSIONS

The following are a number of interesting illusions that create circles from straight lines, tunnels from spirals, color from black and white. Each illusion is achieved by copying the pattern onto white paper or a white paper plate and spinning the pattern at different speeds. Try mounting the patterns on an **Optical Spinner** (page 93) or an **Optical Twirler** (page 94).

These illusions appear at various speeds and lighting, so you and your child may have to experiment a bit.

● OPTICAL SPINNER

You need: Plastic cover from soft margarine tub or similar container
Lightweight white paper plate *or* white paper
Wooden toothpick
Pin or needle

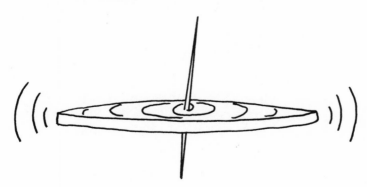

93

You do: (See illustration, page 95.)
               Use pin or needle to poke a hole in center of plastic cover.
                 Hole should be big enough for toothpick to fit snugly.
               Insert toothpick in hole, as shown.

Child does: To spin top, child spins long end of toothpick between
                 thumb and forefinger.

Note: Child should *practice* with blank Spinner before trying
                 optical illusions.

How to   Cut paper into circle slightly smaller than plastic cover.
mount   Copy optical illusion pattern onto paper (see pages 97–
optical   99).
illusions on Poke hole in center of pattern and mount on spinner by
Spinner: sliding pattern over toothpick and fitting into plastic
                 cover.

■   **OPTICAL TWIRLER**

You need: Plastic cover from soft margarine, canned food, etc. (ap-
                 proximately 3–4 inches in diameter.)
               Nail
               Lightweight string, yarn, or heavy thread—4 feet long

You do: (See illustration, opposite)
               Locate the center of the cover and poke two holes, as
                 shown, about ¼–½ inch apart. (1)

You and   Thread string or yarn through holes, as shown, and tie a
child do: knot to form a large loop. (2)

Child does: Moves plastic cover to center of string.
               Holds string as shown in Figure 3, and twirls plastic cover
                 about thirty times, so that string (or yarn) is wound
                 tightly.
               Gentle pull and release of tension will make plastic cover
                 spin to unwind and wind repeatedly. The trick is to
                 bring hands slightly together as cord winds up, and
                 draw hands apart as cord unwinds. (4)

Note: Child should *practice* with blank Twirler before trying
                 optical illusions.

94

(1)

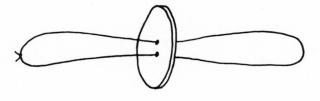

(2)

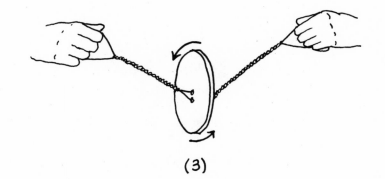

(3)

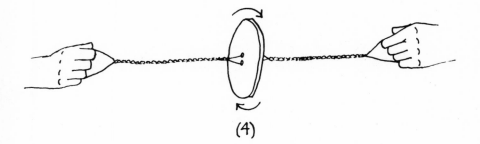

(4)

How to
mount
optical
illusions on
Twirler:

(See illustration, below.)
Copy illusion and cut paper into a circle slightly smaller than plastic cover. (1)
Locate exact center of illusion pattern. Cut a slit from outside to slightly beyond center of paper, as shown. (2)
Slide paper over strings and secure with clear tape. (3)
If desired, mount two different illusions at the same time (one on each side), so that two illusions can be observed during one spin.

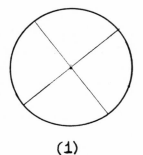 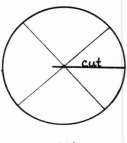

(1)   (2)

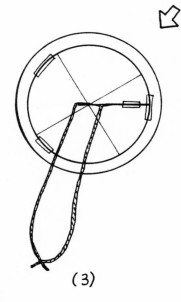

(3)

■ THE ILLUSIONS

(Use the following procedure to try any or all of the illusions described on pages 93–94.)

You need: White paper plate or white paper
Ruler or straight edge
Pencil
Black felt-tipped pen or thin marker
Colored markers
Scissors
Clear tape
Optical Spinner or Optical Twirler

You and   Using a pencil, copy the patterns onto white paper or a
child do: white paper plate. When they are just right, carefully go
over the patterns with very black marker.
Mount on **Optical Spinner** or **Optical Twirler,** page
93 and page 94.

Tunnels from Spirals

Circles from Straight Lines

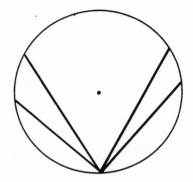

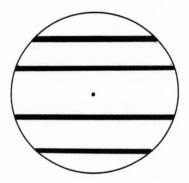

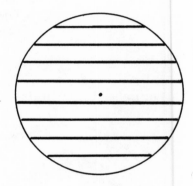

Color from Black and White

Note: This illusion uses a device called a Benham disk. The patterns for these disks are most easily copied by first dividing your circles evenly, as shown in Figure 1.

The illusion works best in bright light. You and your child will have to experiment with different light and spinning speeds, but eventually you should see flashes of color. If using an Optical Twirler, you should spin the disk rather *slowly* for the best result.

Reversing the direction of spin will cause the colors to change places!

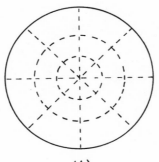

(1)

BENHAM DISKS

99

Color Mixers

Note: Your child may want to experiment with different patterns and color combinations of his/her own.

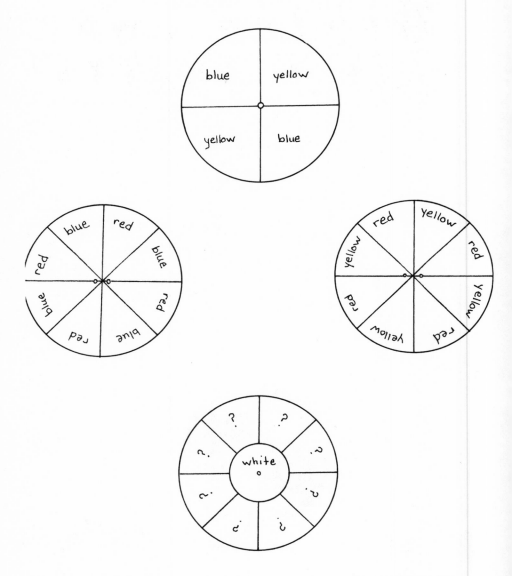

See also: **Toothpick Structures,** page 68, for an activity with three-dimensional structures; **Creature Count,** page 193, and **Star Gazing,** page 198, for outdoor science.

SEWING AND FABRIC CRAFTS

YARN CRAFTS

● SEW-A-PICTURE

You need: Thin cardboard (Good sources: poster board, paper plates, cardboard insert from tights or shirt package, large index cards)
Markers or crayons
Large needle
Yarn or embroidery thread (Different colors are nicest.)

Child does: (See illustration.)
Draws a simple line drawing on cardboard.
Using a running stitch or overcast stitch (page 107), child stitches a frame around the outer edge of the drawing.
Using a different color yarn (if available), child stitches an outline around the larger objects in the drawing (e.g., house, boat, plane, sun, etc.).
Child then colors drawing with markers or crayons.

YARN DOLLS

You need: Yarn

Scissors

A book about 4–6 inches across (or a similar size piece of
sturdy cardboard)

You and
child do: (See illustration.)

Cut six pieces of yarn, each 8 inches long, and set aside to
use for tying.

Loosely wrap yarn around book about 25 times. Use a
separate piece of yarn to tie bundle together at the top.
You can tie a bow, if desired. (1)

Slide yarn off book and tie about 1 inch from the top, to
form the head. (2)

Wrap more yarn around the book about 12 times. Slide
yarn off book and use separate pieces of yarn to tie
bundle in middle and at each end, forming arms and
hands. (3)

Insert arms through center of yarn "body," just below the
head, and tie as shown, to form waist. (4)

If doll is wearing skirt, cut bottom loops and trim ends
evenly.

If doll is wearing pants, separate yarn into two parts, and
use two more short lengths of yarn to tie at bottom,
forming feet. (5)

Optional: Add colorful "clothing" by winding contrasting color yarn
around doll's arms and legs. (6)

Ideas: Make red and green yarn dolls (about 4 or 5 inches high)
to hang on your Christmas tree.

Make a yarn doll mobile.

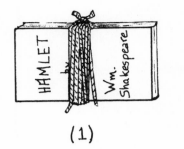

(1)

(3)

(5)

(2)

(4)

(6)

■ POM-POMS

You need: Yarn
Scissors
Sturdy cardboard 3 inches across

You and
child do: (See illustration.)
Loosely wrap yarn around cardboard about 100 times! If using lightweight yarn, wrap as many as 200 times. (1)
Slide roll of yarn off cardboard and use a separate piece of yarn to tie the roll tightly in the middle. (2)
Cut all the loops and trim to form ball shape. (3)

Idea: Glue bits of felt or construction paper to outside surface of pom-pom to make **pom-pom creatures.** (4)

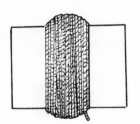

(1)

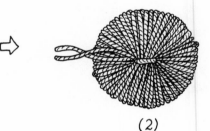

(2)

(3)

(4)

SEWING CRAFTS

●■   BASIC STITCHES

The following crafts use one or two of these basic stitches.

Running Stitch
Young children will find this stitch easiest to use.

Reinforced Running Stitch
After completing a section of running stitches, reverse your sewing direction and fill in the spaces.

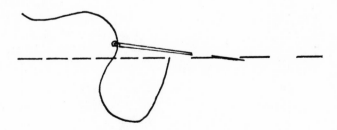

Back Stitch

Older children may want to try a back stitch, which needs no reinforcement.

Overcast Stitch (Whipstitch)

Another simple stitch.

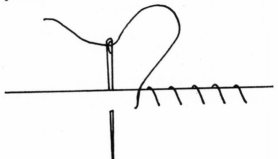

The fabric for these crafts needn't be new. (A worn-out sweatshirt might make a perfect pillow or stuffed animal.) Use fabric cut from old clothes or leftovers from a larger sewing project. Or you can make a trip to a fabric store's remnant pile.

■ TOOTH PILLOW

You need: 2 squares of fabric, slightly larger than desired pillow size (Lightweight fabric is best. A 5-inch square is a nice size to start with.)
1 square of fabric, 2 × 2 inches (Felt is easiest to work with.)
Needle and thread
Scissors
Straight pins
Stuffing material (cotton balls, shredded nylon stockings, polyester stuffing, etc.)
Markers (optional)

You and   (See illustration.)

child do: Pin small fabric square to center of *right side* of one large square, as shown. Stitch along three sides of small square (running stitch or overcast stitch) to make pocket. (1)

With *right sides together,* pin and then stitch large fabric squares together, using reinforced running stitch or backstitch. Leave a 2–3-inch space on one edge. (2)

Turn right side out.

Fill with stuffing material and sew pillow closed, using an overcast stitch. (3)

Child does: Decorates with markers, if desired. Leaves baby tooth in tiny pocket for Tooth Fairy.

Tooth Fairy Leaves reward in pocket, to be found the next **does:**   morning!

(1)

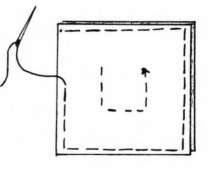

(2)

(3)

■ SHAPE PILLOW

You need: Fabric (Light- or medium-weight fabric is best.)
Needle and thread
Scissors
Straight pins
Stuffing material (polyester stuffing, old, shredded nylon stockings, etc.)
Paper and pencil

Child does: (See illustration.)
Decides on desired shape of pillow and draws a pattern on paper. (Some shapes to try: heart, arrow, crescent moon, round with button in center, tulip, triangle, etc.) (1)

You and child do: Fold fabric in half with right sides together, and pin pattern. Cut around pattern, *leaving ½-inch border.* (2)
Remove pattern and sew around edges of fabric, leaving ½-inch seam allowance. Use reinforced running stitch or backstitch. Leave a 2–3-inch space on one edge. (3)
Use scissors to trim seams and clip fabric at sharp turns. (4)
Turn pillow right side out. Check seams for holes and mend them. Check pillow's shape, and make adjustments if necessary. Stuff firmly with stuffing.
Sew pillow closed, using overcast stitch. (5)

(1)

(2)

(3)   (4)

(5)

■ SACHETS

You need: Fabric (Lightweight is best.)
Needle and thread
Scissors
Straight pins
Stuffing material: **Simple Potpourri** (see page 191)
Or
Polyester stuffing, old stockings, cotton balls, etc., that
have been *lightly scented* with a few drops of perfume.

You and   Follow directions for **Shape Pillow,** page 110. (Sachets
child do: can be simple squares or fancier shapes.)
Fill loosely with scented potpourri or other scented stuffing material.
Sew closed using overcast stitch.
Child may want to decorate sachet with bits of ribbon or
lace.

▲ EASY STUFFED ANIMALS

You need: Fabric (Soft fabric is nicest. Avoid slippery fabric, which is hard to work with, and fabric that is very thin or very stiff. Corduroy, flannel, velour, and soft knits work well.)
Needle and thread
Scissors
Straight pins
Paper and pencil
Buttons (for eyes)
Yarn or embroidery thread (for nose and mouth)
Stuffing material (polyester stuffing or shredded nylon stockings)

Child does: (See illustrations, pages 113 and 114.)
Decides what kind of stuffed animal to make, and *draws a sketch* of his/her idea. This drawing needn't be fancy, but it will be a guide as to the size, shape, and detail of the finished product. (1)
Chooses fabric.

You and child do: On a separate piece of paper, make a pattern by drawing a larger version of child's original sketch. Allow for ½-inch seams *on all edges.* You may want to even up proportions if necessary (e.g., make arms and legs equal in length, give animal slightly bigger ears, etc.) (2)

Child does: Cuts out paper pattern. (2)

You and child do: Fold fabric in half, with right sides together. Pin pattern to fabric. Cut out pattern. (3)

Child does: Chooses one piece of the cutout fabric to be the front of the animal. Uses a marker or pencil to mark position of eyes, nose, and mouth on right side of fabric.

You and child do: Sew on eyes (buttons), nose (button, yarn, or embroidery thread), and mouth (yarn or embroidery thread). (4)
With *right sides together,* pin front and back together. Sew around edges of fabric, leaving ½-inch seam allowance.

(1)

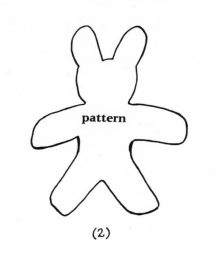

pattern

(2)

(3)

(4)

Use reinforced running stitch or backstitch. Be sure to *leave a 2–3-inch space open* to add stuffing. (5)

Use scissors to trim seams and clip fabric at sharp curves. (6)

Child does: Turns stuffed animal right side out. Checks to make sure the eyes, nose, and mouth are positioned correctly. Checks for holes in seams.

Stuffs animal with stuffing material. (Be sure that the ears, arms, and legs are as well packed as the rest of the body.)

You and child do: Use an overcast stitch to close opening. (7)

(5)

(6)

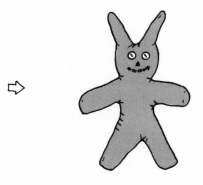

(7)

■ POUCH

You need: Light- to medium-weight fabric, 7 × 10 inches (Try to use fabric that doesn't fray at the edges too much.)
Needle and thread
Straight pins
Piece of yarn or thin ribbon, 28 inches long
Scissors
Something to thread ribbon through pouch (chopstick, knitting needle, long pencil, etc.)
Tape

You and child do: (See illustration, pages 116 and 117.)
Lay fabric right side down. (1)
Fold top, long edge of fabric down 1 inch and pin. Use reinforced running stitch or backstitch to sew edge down, forming "tunnel." (2)
Tape one end of ribbon or yarn to one end of chopstick, pencil, etc., and thread ribbon through fabric tunnel. (3)
Fold fabric in half, *right sides together* as shown, and pin edges. Use reinforced running stitch or backstitch to sew sides of pouch. (4) *Do not* sew through ribbon, but try to sew as high on sides of pouch as you can.
Tie ends of ribbon or yarn together.
Turn pouch right side out. (5)

Easy Variation: If your piece of fabric does not fray *or* if a long edge of your fabric is a bias edge, omit steps 2 and 3. (6)
Fold fabric, right sides together, so that bias edge forms top of pouch. Pin and sew bottom and side together, as shown. (7)
Turn pouch right side out.
Thread yarn on needle and stitch a loose running stitch around top of pouch, ½ inch down from the bias edge. (8)
Tie ends of yarn. (9)

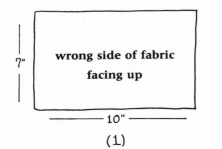

7"

wrong side of fabric facing up

10"

(1)

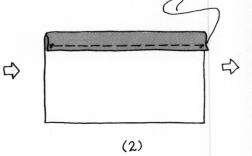

(2)

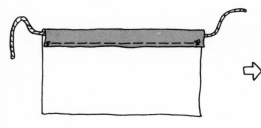

(3)

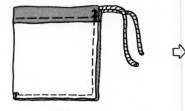

(4)

(5)

Easy Variation

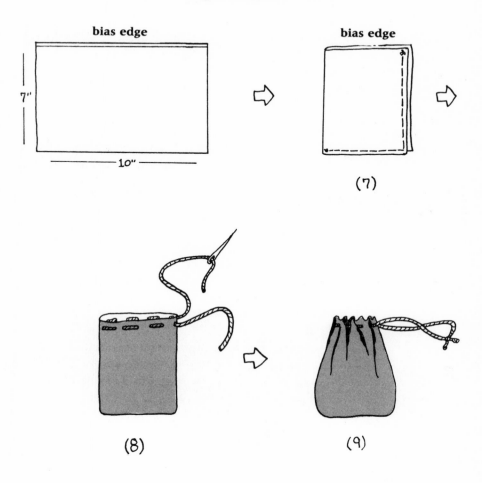

bias edge

7"

10"

bias edge

(7)

(8)

(9)

Pouch Necklace Variation:	Follow directions above, but use a smaller piece of material and a longer piece of ribbon or yarn. Tiny pouch is worn as a necklace, holding a lucky charm or some other small and special item.
Note:	Before child carries anything in pouch, be sure to check for *holes* in seams!

▲   **MINI-BACKPACK**
         (For a stuffed animal or doll to wear on trips.)

You need: Medium- to heavy-weight fabric, about 5 × 12 inches
              (Denim or old sweatshirt material works well.)
              Needle and thread
              Scissors
              Two pieces of ribbon or elastic, each 4–6 inches long

You and   (See diagram.)
child do: Estimate size of backpack for animal or doll, and cut fabric
                 to approximately the same shape as shown in Figure 1.
              Lay fabric *right side down*. Fold short top and bottom edges
                 over ½ inch and pin. Use a running stitch to sew in
                 place. (2)
              Turn fabric right side up.
              Fold wide end of fabric up about 4 inches. (3)
              Match edges on sides and pin in place. Fabric will bulge
                 slightly to form pouch. Sew sides closed using rein-
                 forced running stitch, backstitch, or overcast stitch. (4)
              There should be about 3–4 inches of fabric at top to act as
                 backpack cover.
              Turn backpack right side out. Use running stitch to hem
                 sides of backpack top, as shown. (5)
              Sew ribbon or elastic on back of pack. Arms of stuffed
                 animal or doll slide through loops. (6)

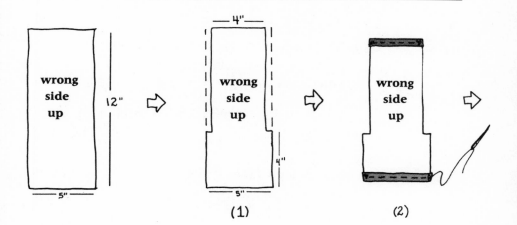

(1)

(2)

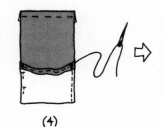

(3)

(4)

(5)

back view

front view

(6)

▲ BELT PACK

You need: Medium- to heavy-weight fabric, 7 × 12 inches (Denim or old sweatshirt material works well.)
Needle and thread
Scissors
Two ribbon or fabric pieces, each 2–3 inches long and ½ inch wide

You and child do: (See diagram.)
Cut fabric to approximately the same shape as shown in Figure 1.
Lay fabric *right side down.* Fold short edges over ½ inch and pin. Use a running stitch to sew in place. (2)
Turn fabric right side up.
Fold wide end of fabric up 3½ inches. (3)
Match edges on sides and pin in place. Fabric will bulge slightly to form pouch. Sew sides closed using reinforced running stitch, backstitch, or overcast stitch. (4)
There should be about 4 inches of fabric at top to act as belt pack cover.
Turn pack right side out. Use running stitch to hem sides of pack top, as shown. (5)
Sew ribbon pieces on back of pack, as shown. (6)
Wear pack on belt. (7)

Optional: Sew a button on inside front of pack, if desired. Cut a small slit in fabric for buttonhole.

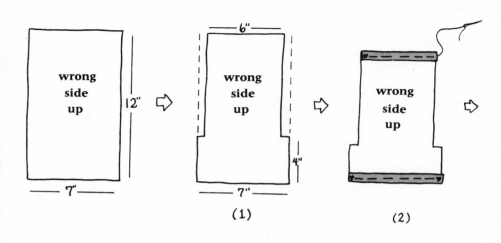

wrong side up · 12"

7"

(1)

6" · wrong side up · 7" · 4"

(2)

wrong side up

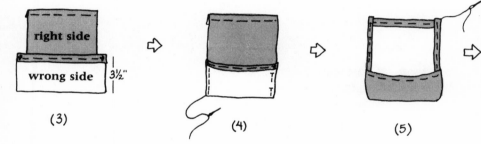

right side · wrong side · 3½"

(3)

(4)

(5)

back view

(6)

front view

CRAYON CRAFTS WITH FABRIC

(Expensive fabric crayons are not required for these crafts!)

You need: Ordinary crayons
Bright markers
White paper
Light-weight fabric (White cotton or muslin work best, although any light-colored fabric should work. Avoid stretchy fabrics, which are difficult to color on.)
Iron
2 paper towels

Child does: Using bright markers, child draws a simple picture on white paper.

You and child do: Lay fabric over drawing. Trace and copy drawing with crayons, directly onto fabric. Make sure crayon colors are bright and filled in.

You do: Set iron on High (cotton) setting.
When iron is hot, place fabric between two paper towels and iron excess crayon out. Finished fabric should be brightly colored and soft.

Note: Older child can draw directly on fabric, if desired, without making preliminary marker drawing.
Crayon fabric crafts can be machine-washed and -dried.

● WALLHANGING

You need: Crayon Craft picture on fabric square or rectangle (see page 122)

Needle and thread

Straight pins

2 thin, straight sticks, slightly longer than the width of your picture (dowels, sticks, chopsticks, bamboo skewers, thin cardboard tube from wire hangers, etc.)

Yarn or string

You and
child do: (See illustration.)

Lay Crayon Craft face down.

Depending on width of sticks you are using, fold 1–2 inches of fabric to back of picture on top and bottom. Pin and sew along edge of fabric with running stitch, to form "tunnel." (1)

Slide sticks through spaces at top and bottom of picture. Tie yarn to ends of top stick and hang. (2)

(1)   (2)

■ PILLOW

You need: Pillow fabric: 2 Crayon Craft pictures (see page 122) of
the same size

Or

1 Crayon Craft picture with a plain fabric piece of the
same size
Needle and thread
Straight pins
Stuffing materials (polyester stuffing, old stockings, etc.)

You and   Using Crayon Craft fabric pieces, follow directions for
child do: **Shape Pillow,** page 110. Be sure to place fabric *right*
sides together before sewing.

Ideas: *Mood Pillow*—Make a circle pillow with a happy face on
one side and a sad face on the other.
Man in the Moon Pillow—Crescent moon pillow with a
profile on each side.
Stop Sign Pillow—Make a white octagon pillow (tricky!)
and write STOP in big red letters.
Name Pillow—Any shape you want, with child's name or
the name of person to receive pillow written on the
front. Try **Lively Lettering,** page 56.

▲ POT HOLDER

You need: Crayon Craft picture (see page 122) on 7-inch square of
fabric
Old bath towel
6-inch ribbon scrap (optional)
Needle and thread
Scissors
Ruler
Straight pins

You and   (See illustration.)
child do: Cut 7 × 14-inch rectangle of bath towel. Fold in half.
Place Crayon Craft square *face down* on doubled towel

124

square and pin together. The folded edge of the towel should be on top. (1)

Use a reinforced running stitch, backstitch, or overcast stitch to sew all the layers together on *three sides. Leave the top edge open.* (2)

Child does: Turns pot holder right side out.

You do: Fold top edges of towel and Crayon Craft in ½ an inch, and pin. (3)

Child does: Uses reinforced running stitch, backstitch, or overcast stitch to sew pot holder closed. (4)

Optional: You may want to sew a loop of ribbon into the corner of your pot holder as you sew it closed. (4)

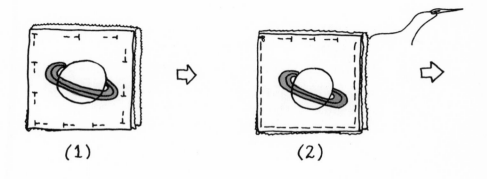

(1)   (2)

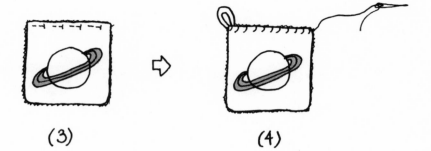

(3)   (4)

EADING CRAFTS

The following three crafts use beads available in craft stores. You will also need a thin beading needle and nylon beading thread.

● SIMPLE BEAD NECKLACE
(An easy necklace for child's early beading projects.)

You need: Beads (2 or 3 different colors)
Beading needle and thread
Scissors
Shallow dish

Child does: (See illustration.)
Decides on colors and pattern of necklace. Child can use paper and markers to design necklace pattern, if desired.
Pours small number of beads on dish. (This minimizes mess if beads spill.)

(1)   (2)

Measures thread to desired necklace length. *Be sure that necklace will be long enough to go over child's head.* Add about 10 inches of extra thread to necklace length, to be sure to have enough thread to tie knots.

Thread needle.

Use needle to pick up 1 bead. Slide bead to end of thread and tie a *secure* knot around bead. This will be one end of necklace. (1)

Continue to pick up beads with needle, following color pattern or randomly. (2)

When necklace is long enough, *securely* tie knot through first bead, to form necklace.

■ **FLOWER BEAD NECKLACE**

You need: Beads (3 different colors)
Beading needle and thread
Scissors
Shallow dish

Child does: Decides on colors and pattern of flower necklace. Child can use paper and markers to design necklace pattern, if desired.

You and child do: (See illustration.)
Follow preparation steps as in **Simple Bead Necklace, page 126.**
Flower necklace is a series of 8-bead flowers, separated by a string of 10 beads.
Thread 10 beads of color #1. (1)
Thread 7 beads of color #2. (2)

(1)   (2)

Bring needle through first bead of color #2, forming a circle. (Figures 3 and 4)

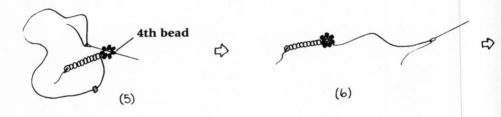

(3)　　　　　**4th bead**　　　(4)

Thread one bead of color #3. Bring needle through *fourth* bead of color #2, as shown. (5) This single bead forms the center of the flower. (6)

4th bead

(5)　　　　　　　　　(6)

Now thread 10 beads of color #1 again. (7)
Repeat steps 2–7 until necklace is desired length.
Securely tie knot to finish necklace. (8)

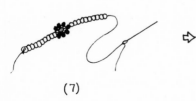

(7)

(8)

▲ **INDIAN BEAD NECKLACE**
    (This is a good adult-child project.)

You need: Beads (3 different colors)
            Beading thread and 2 needles
            Scissors
            Shallow dish

Child does: Decides on colors and pattern of Indian necklace. Child
              can use paper and markers to design necklace pattern,
              if desired.

You and   (See illustration.)
child do: Indian Bead Necklace is a double strand of beads, con-
            nected at regular intervals by a single bead.
            Follow preparation steps as in **Simple Bead Necklace,**
            page 126, but cut *two* lengths of thread.
            Pour a small number of beads onto plate.
            Thread both threads through a color #1 bead and securely
            tie both threads to it, as shown.

Thread 2 beads of color #2 on each thread.

Thread 8 beads of color #3 on each thread.

Thread 2 beads of color #2 on each thread.

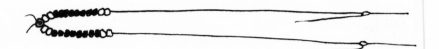

Thread *both* threads through a *single* color #1 bead. (Avoid running needle through strands of thread.)

Thread 2 beads of color #2 on each thread.

Thread 8 beads of color #3 on each thread.
Continue threading beads in this pattern until necklace is complete.

Securely tie knot to finish necklace.

Variations: Your child can design an infinite number of necklaces, using different colors, patterns, and sizes of beads. The pictured example is only a start.

WRITING AND THINKING

● **TIME CAPSULE**

You need: Symbols of *who your child is right now:* snapshot, height and weight, handwriting sample, typical drawing, label from favorite food item, favorite candy wrapper, important magazine or newspaper articles, list of child's current favorite activities, habits, friends, colors, etc.

Could also include a short letter from relative or friend about what child is like. Child could write or dictate list of hopes and goals for the future (e.g., "What I want to be when I grow up," "What I think the future will be like," etc.).

Sturdy container to store things in: cardboard box with lid, large oatmeal box, shoe box, etc. If humidity is a problem in your area, seal items in a plastic bag before storing them in container.

Aluminum foil (optional)

Masking tape

Markers

Child does: Decides what items go in Time Capsule.

Collects items.

Decorates container. Covering container with aluminum foil gives it a nice "futuristic" look.

Loads items in Time Capsule.

You and child do: Seal Time Capsule with masking tape or twine. Clearly mark outside of container:

TIME CAPSULE!
Property of: Child's Name
Sealed: Date
Do Not Open Until: Date in Future

Note: This future date depends on child's age and enthusiasm for the activity. A waiting period of even one day may

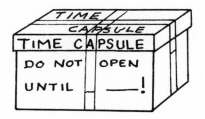

133

be too long for some children. A waiting period of one year may be fine for an older child. Let your child decide how long to wait.

Hide the Time Capsule in an out-of-the-way spot, away from humidity and family activity: attic, high shelf of parents' closet, in box of next season's clothing, etc.

Special Note to Teachers: This might be a good class project for the first week of school. Time Capsules can then be opened and discussed during the last week of school in June.

● MAKE A SCRAPBOOK

You need: Spiral notebook (used or new), or photo album (used or new), or homemade book bound with yarn or string
Magazines with colorful pictures
Markers or crayons
Tape or glue
Scissors

Child does: Decides what kinds of things should go in his/her scrapbook. Child can stick to a theme: ballet, baseball, horses, dogs, sports, fashion, poetry, favorite comic strips, drawings, postcards, poems, observations about life, etc. Or scrapbook can be a collection of all of the above and more.

Decorates cover, as well as filling pages. (Collage makes a nice scrapbook cover.)

■ MAKE A POSTER

(A great way for your child to personalize his/her room.)

You need: Poster board, large paper, or smaller paper taped together.
Magazines with colorful pictures
Markers
Tape or glue
Scissors

Child does: Decides on theme for poster: music, sports, animals, teddy bears, environment, antidrugs, funny, "All about Child's Name," etc.

Fills poster with collage of cutout pictures, drawings, calligraphy, etc. Spaces between pictures can be filled with colored stars, arrows, lines, glitter, or stickers. Pictures can be emphasized by mounting first on contrasting colored paper and then on poster.

Note: If poster theme is environmental, antidrugs, etc., child might consider possibility of hanging it in school, a local store window, community center, etc. (Ask permission first.)

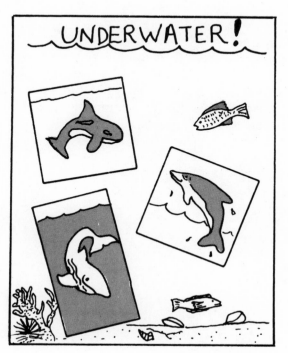

START A COLLECTION

(These collectibles are free or almost free.)

Bags

Watch for unique-looking bags from department or novelty stores. Bags can be plastic or paper, with designs, printing, or both. Child can collect bags of all sizes, or specialize in small bags to conserve space. This is an easy collection to add to. A trip to the mall or a trip to a foreign country will both result in new and different bags!

Napkins

Collect clean paper napkins with restaurant logos or designs on them.

Coasters

Collect paper or cardboard coasters from various restaurants, hotels, etc. Adults may be the best source for these coasters, which are free.

Fortune Cookie Fortunes

Save any and all fortunes from trips to Chinese restaurants, or be selective and save only the very best.

Candy Wrappers

This is a fun and tasty collection! Make sure the wrappers are *clean*. Try to keep them as smooth and new looking as possible. Children can collect from friends or relatives. Try to find *unusual* wrappers, foreign wrappers, etc. Sometimes the candy companies change their packaging, making your *old* wrappers unique.

Bags

A starship ride has been promised to you by the Galactic Wizard.

Fortune Cookie Fortunes

"Strange but True" Articles from the Newspaper

Adults can alert child to these usually brief articles in the newspaper. Child can cut them out, date them, and mount them in a scrapbook as proof that the world is often a strange and funny place. This is also a fun way for children to start reading the newspaper.

Autographs

Collect autographs in a special autograph book, a notebook, or scrapbook. Child collects autographs from friends, relatives, teachers, visiting artists, performers in local productions, athletes in local games. Child may want to write to favorite celebrities and ask for their autographs. Many, but not all, will respond.

Theme Drawings or Pictures

Your child may want to start a collection of his or her own drawings on one particular theme (rocket ships, horses, dogs, outer space, dragons, castles, boats, etc.). Or child can cut out and collect magazine pictures about one theme (sports, rainbows, superheroes, sunsets, fashion, rock stars, sports cars, etc.) Store these pictures in a scrapbook.

Commemorative Postage Stamps

These are stamps with especially pretty pictures on them. Child carefully removes commemorative stamps from family's *incoming* mail. (Soak stamps in water for about one minute. Peel stamps off envelopes and let dry on paper towel.) Encourage friends and relatives to use commemorative stamps when writing to the family.

Foreign Stamps and/or Foreign Coins

A nice gift from a world-traveling friend or relative.

Candy Wrappers

Commemorative stamps

Postcards

Child can organize postcards by location or type (e.g., joke cards, animal cards, landscapes, etc.).

Airline Baggage Tags

Another nice reason to have the family's traveler return home!

Matchbook Covers

A collection from different locations, and/or with pretty designs. Save only the cover, not the matches!

Buttons

Unusual buttons can often be found at rummage sales or on old clothes.

Pennies

Child collects pennies from different years, or just collects lots of pennies in a big jar.

Rocks

Encourage child to start in his/her own backyard or neighborhood, collecting small specimens of common rocks. Watch for new specimens while traveling. Find books in the library to help identify rock samples. Or child may want to collect rocks for their beauty alone. (Try a collection of perfectly round rocks, or beautifully striped ones.) Inexpensive samples of unusual rocks are often available at museum gift shops.

Shells

On family's next trip to the beach, child can search for different types of shells, or collect shells and shell fragments for their beauty alone. Your local library will have books to help identify shells.

Sea Glass

Bits of glass that have been tossed around in the sand and waves for a long time have smooth, rounded edges and a frosty appearance. If you live near the ocean, hunting for sea glass can be like searching for treasure.

Beach Sand

Children will be surprised to see the differences in sand from different locations. Some examples include red sand from Wyoming or

Texas; white sand from Carmel, California; tiny polished pebbles from Bend, Oregon; tiny crushed seashells and urchin spines from Bar Harbor, Maine; black sand with coral chips from Hawaii; coarse sand, fine sand, etc. Label and store the sand samples in clear, reclosable plastic bags or plastic hobby jars.

Feathers

Every so often, as you're walking outdoors, you may discover a fallen bird feather. If it's clean and in good condition, save it for a collection. Use a bird book from the library to identify your feathers. See how many different kinds of birds are represented in your collection.

Mounting or storing your collection:

Store flat things like candy wrappers, coasters, stamps, etc., in spiral notebooks, old picture albums, or books purchased especially for collections. To see both sides of the item, make a "pocket" out of plastic wrap, and tape the open edge to the notebook page. Clear plastic report covers, cut to size, make good pockets, too. Child can then label each item.

Store three-dimensional things like rocks, shells, or buttons on a piece of stiff cardboard or in a shallow box. (A gift box is good.) Use a ruler and pencil or marker to divide the base into even squares. Child can then label each square and glue down specimens, if desired.

Buttons

Shells

Feathers

WORD SEARCHES WITH A THEME

You need: Paper
Pencil
Ruler

You and   Child decides on a theme for word search (e.g., animals,
child do: planets, family names, colors, sports, toys, holidays,
etc.).

You do: (See example.)
Use ruler to make a grid, 10 squares by 10 squares (larger
for older child; smaller for younger child).
Fill grid with words relating to theme, spelling words
forwards, backwards, up and down, and diagonally.
List words below grid. (1)
Fill empty spaces on grid with random letters. (2)

Ideas: You can make word search for child, while child makes
word search for you.
Two children can make their own word searches and then
trade.

G		B	A	S	E	B	A	L	L
	O		H	O	C	K	E	Y	L
		L		C			K		A
			F	C			C		B
S	I	N	N	E	T		A		T
				R			R		E
							T		K
			G	N	I		I	K	S
	F	O	O	T	B	A	L	L	A
G	N	I	M	M	I	W	S		B

BASEBALL   GOLF
HOCKEY   SOCCER
TENNIS   TRACK
BASKETBALL
SKIING   FOOTBALL
SWIMMING

(1)

G	Z	B	A	S	E	B	A	L	L
P	O	T	H	O	C	K	E	Y	L
Q	S	L	M	C	R	L	K	S	A
D	A	A	F	C	V	S	C	I	B
S	I	N	N	E	T	A	A	D	T
R	L	A	H	R	W	M	R	T	E
L	N	P	C	E	H	U	T	J	K
E	G	F	R	G	N	I	I	K	S
C	F	O	O	T	B	A	L	L	A
G	N	I	M	M	I	W	S	Y	B

BASEBALL   GOLF
HOCKEY   SOCCER
TENNIS   TRACK
BASKETBALL
SKIING   FOOTBALL
SWIMMING

(2)

ESP GAME

(A game of Extrasensory Perception)

You need: 8 index cards (or 8 pieces of white paper, 3 × 3 inches)
Markers

Child does: (See example.)
Draws a square on 2 cards.
Draws a circle on 2 cards.
Draws a triangle on 2 cards.
Draws a star on 2 cards.
Colors in shapes, if desired.

Note: Make sure that pairs of shapes are as *identical* as possible.

You and
child do: Each person has a set of four cards, laid out face up, in front of him/her. Sit so that you can't see each other's cards.

One person is the "Sender." The other person is the "Receiver."

The Sender picks up one card and concentrates on the shape, either by thinking about it, staring at it, or tracing it with a finger.

The Receiver tries to concentrate and guess, by receiving a mental message, what the Sender's chosen shape is. When the Receiver thinks of the shape, he/she picks up the card and shows it to the Sender. The Sender tells the Receiver if the choice was correct or not.

Note: Take turns being Sender and Receiver. This is a noncompetitive game that adults can play with children, or that two children can play together.

If ESP isn't working well, increase the odds by working with only three pairs of cards!

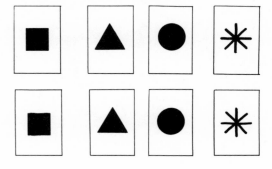

▲ MAKE YOUR OWN BOARD GAME

You need: Poster board is best (or use cardboard, large paper, or small paper taped together)

Markers or crayons

Dice, homemade spinner, and/or homemade cards (see below)

Game piece for each player (buttons, pennies, pebbles, etc.)

Note: The simplest approach is to design a game in which players take turns traveling through dangerous territory toward a reward or goal. Along the way, players encounter setbacks, shortcuts, and bonuses. The first player to reach the goal wins the game.

Child does: Decides on theme for the game. Examples:

● Searching through a castle for a magic charm while being chased by dragons.

● Searching for pirate treasure on a booby-trapped island.

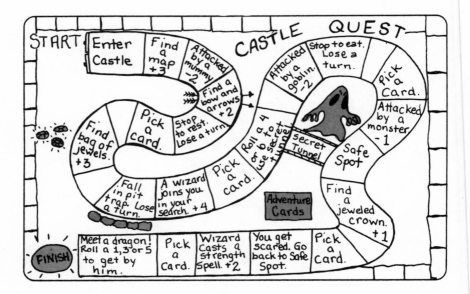

● Running a marathon race while coping with bad weather, traffic, potholes, fatigue, muscle cramps, dehydration.

● Traveling through force fields and hostile galaxies to a distant planet, in order to save an alien population!

You and child do: Design game board. (See examples.) Path of travel should be broken up into spaces.

Simple games should have directions written directly in spaces on game board. (It's okay to leave some spaces blank.)

More elaborate game will direct player to "pick a card from Adventure Pile." These Adventure Cards will describe a player's predicament (e.g., "You are locked in a dungeon. Miss one turn." "A winged horse gives you a lift. Go ahead three spaces").

Decorate game board with related drawings (e.g., palm trees, outer space, green grass and flowers, etc.).

Players throw a die to determine how many spaces to advance. If a die is not available, make a spinner, or make a stack of cards numbered 1 through 6, which players can shuffle and pick.

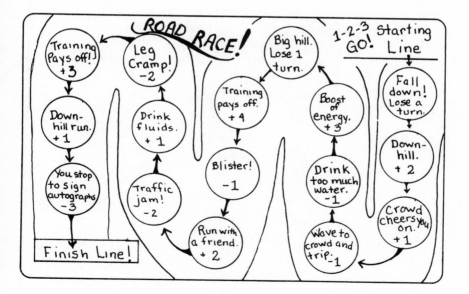

■ CODES

You need: Paper
              Pencils

You and   Make up a code or codes substituting letters, numbers, or
child do: symbols for the regular alphabet.

Ideas: Write out an alphabet key so that messages can be
              decoded easily.

                              Or

              Write out the *rule* by which the code was made. For
              example: "A = 1, B = 2, and so on." *Or* "Add three
              letters to each letter, as in A = D, B = E, and so on."

                              Or

Keep the code a secret from the child, giving only a small
hint as to the rule. Child must then try to crack the
code.

Examples:

● Write the child's full name in code.

● Give away the first six to ten letters in code, but
don't explain the rule.

● Tell the child what all the vowels are in code, but
none of the consonants.

● Give no hints at all, but suggest that child try to
crack code by paying attention to certain patterns:

—common letter groupings: th, sh, st

—single letter words: I, A

—common short, recurring words: the, and, it, to,
but

—most popular vowels: a, e, i, o

Tap out or write messages using Morse code (see below).

A ·—	B —···	C —·—·	D —··	E ·
F ··—·	G ——·	H ····	I ··	J ·———
K —·—	L ·—··	M ——	N —·	O ———
P ·——·	Q ——·—	R ·—·	S ···	T —
U ··—	V ···—	W ·——	X —··—	Y —·——
Z ——··				

▲ MAPS

You need: Paper
         Pencils

You and   ● (See Map #1, page 146.) Map a neighborhood (real or
child do: imaginary). Label roads, buildings, landmarks. While child
         colors in and decorates map, you write a list of directions
         for child to follow on an imaginary walk, such as:
   1. Start at our house. Turn left and go to corner.
   2. Turn left at corner and go two blocks.
   3. Turn right and go one block.
   4. Turn left and go one block.
   5. Turn right and go one block.
   6. Turn right and walk almost two blocks.
   7. Stop at the last building on the right. Where are
      you?
   Answer: *Library*

   ● (See Map #2, page 147.) Do above mapping activity,
   but use directions (North, South, East, and West) and
   street names in clues. Include compass rose on map.
   Sample instructions might be:
   1. Start on the west corner of Rodeo Drive and Main
      Street, and go south for one block.
   2. Turn west onto Coral Drive and go one block.
   3. Travel south one block.
   4. Turn east, and travel until you get to Ivy Lane.
   5. Turn north onto Ivy Lane, then east onto Coral
      Drive, to Broadway.
   6. Travel south on Broadway for two blocks, cross the
      street, and enter the driveway. What are you late
      for?
   Answer: *School*

   ● Do above map activity using a section of a real city
   map. *Or* use tourist maps, which are free in many
   areas or are found on paper placemats in some
   restaurants.
   ● Draw a simple map of the route from your house to
   the store, a friend's house, school, a local park, etc.
   Drive, ride bikes, or walk this route with your child,

145

stopping occasionally to check your progress on the map.

- Before going on a long trip, use a highlighter to mark your route on a road map. Your child can follow your progress, watch for upcoming town names, rivers, lakes, etc.
- Also see **Backyard Orienteering Treasure Hunt,** page 201.

MAP #1

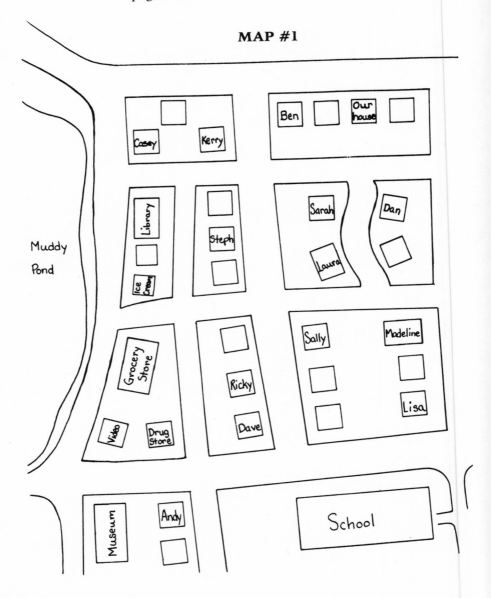

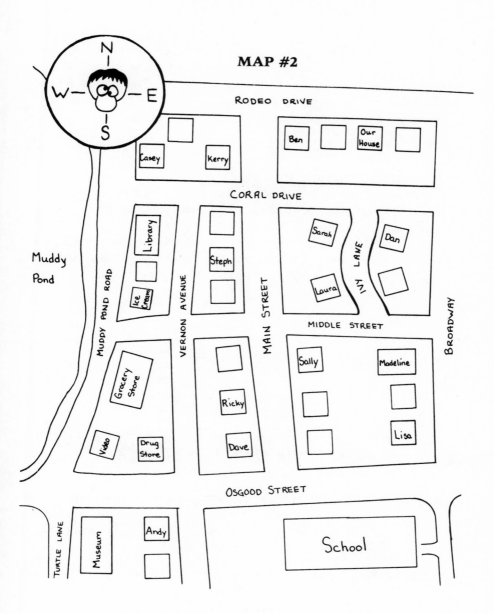

MAP #2

◼ WRITE TO YOUR FAVORITE MAGAZINE

Most magazines have a section for "Letters from Readers." Your child may want to express an opinion, and it's fun to see your name in print. Encourage your child to write a short letter to a favorite magazine, and then watch for the letter over the next few months. The address for the magazine should be on the Letters page.

Here's an easy form to follow when writing a letter.

Today's Date

Dear Name of Magazine,
    Your child can voice an opinion about the magazine as a whole, or talk about a particular article. On a more personal note, children may want to describe favorite hobbies, sports, or interests. The letter should be fairly short, and should relate to the magazine's topic. For instance, when writing to a nature magazine, the letter might be about camping, hiking, the environment, etc.

Sincerely,

Child's Name
(Child's Age)

▲ WRITE YOUR OWN NEWSPAPER
(This is a fun group or family activity.)

You need: Pencils and scrap paper for taking notes and writing rough drafts
Paper for the final draft (8½ × 11 inches or larger)
Typewriter or word processor (optional)

Child does: Your child (and his/her friends) can be editor, reporter, cartoonist, movie or book reviewer, sportswriter, advice columnist, or just a few of the above.

You do: Younger children may need help writing the articles.
Younger children may hire you to type, word-process, or print the final draft. Older children may prefer to do this themselves.

Ideas: (See example.)

Newspaper Name—Goofy Gazette, <u>Family Name</u> Herald, etc.

Headlines—"Dave Cleans Room, Finds 4-Year-Old Sandwich!" or "Gerbil Loose in Sister's Room!"

Current Events—follow-up on headlines; family issues, school events, etc.

Interviews—"Up Close and Personal with the Family Dog" or "My Best Friend—What Makes Him Tick?"

Book, TV Show, or Movie Reviews

Restaurant Reviews/Meal Reviews—"Dad proved once again that he can turn any food into a casserole when . . ."

Advice Column—Can be pretend problems (funny or serious) or true-to-life problems. Make a "Dear <u>Child's Name</u>" mailbox for anonymous letters.

Games—Word searches, crossword puzzles, etc.

Comics Section

Artworks—drawings, snapshots

Note: If newspaper turns out to be a masterpiece, you might consider making copies so you have some to give away.

A holiday newspaper might feature articles highlighting the family's past year. Copies can be sent to distant friends and relatives.

■ SONG WRITING

You need: Paper
Pencil
Lots of imagination

Child does: Your child (and his/her friends) can make up new and imaginative lyrics to popular songs of today, to old favorites, or to nursery rhymes. Write down the new lyrics (including the original song title so you know the correct tune). Store these lyrics in a notebook or scrapbook with an appropriately silly cover and lots of illustrations.

Examples: Sung to "Row, Row, Row Your Boat"

Tow, tow, tow your goat
out into the yard.
Feed him watermelon rinds.
It isn't very hard!

Or

No! No! No's my vote!
I will not go to school.
I'll stay at home and watch TV
and grow up to be a fool!

QUICK AND EASY COSTUMES

FORTUNE TELLER, SUPER HERO, AND ROCK STAR

PIRATE, MUMMY, AND HIPPIE

Quick costumes come in handy for Halloween, school productions, or just for fun. See **Accessories,** page 168, for more costume ideas.

◖ GYPSY/FORTUNE TELLER

Child wears **Kerchief,** page 174, on head, and *lots* of jewelry (see **Silver Bead Necklace,** page 168). Girls wear makeup, long skirt, blouse, and shawl. Tuck colorful scarves into waistband of skirt, hanging by one corner, and secure with safety pins. Boys wear bright shirt, vest, and dark pants. Tie a brightly colored scarf around child's waist, leaving the ends hanging.

"Crystal ball" can be play ball wrapped in aluminum foil, covered with plastic wrap, and secured with clear tape.

Children can offer to read palms, or tell fortunes from a deck of cards. ("You will get homework sometime in the next few days." "You will sneeze at least three times this week.")

▲ SUPERHERO

This can be a traditional superhero or someone from your child's imagination. A sweatshirt or long underwear top is perfect for this. Help your child draw the superhero emblem on paper and then transfer the pattern to the appropriate color felt. Sew or glue (with water-soluble white glue) the felt emblem to the front of the sweatshirt or underwear top.

Attach a similar emblem to the back of a **Cape,** page 170.

Gloves (see page 174), a **Belt** (see page 174), and a mask complete the effect.

● ROCK STAR

Mousse or gel in hair for punk styles. Lots of makeup for both boys and girls. Depending on clothing available and type of "rock," child can wear flashy, shiny outfit; ripped up, painted T-shirt and jeans; or go for the clean-cut look. Make life-size cutout of guitar from heavy cardboard. Decorate with paints or markers. Hang around neck with ribbon or old necktie.

■ PIRATE
(This costume makes good use of torn clothing!)

Child wears **Kerchief,** page 174, eye patch, shirt or sweatshirt, and torn pants, sweatpants, or **Quick Knickers,** page 173. Belt can be either a plain belt with a big buckle or a scarf wrapped around child's waist. Tuck a plastic or cardboard sword or pistol into belt. Complete the look with a hoop **Earring,** page 174, on one ear, and perhaps an eyebrow pencil scar on one cheek.

■ MUMMY

Child wears sweatsuit. Tear old sheet into long strips, 2–3 inches wide. Wrap strips loosely and sloppily around torso, arms, and legs, securing ends of strips to sweatsuit with a couple of stitches. Leave some ends hanging, raggedly. Tie ragged headband around child's head. Dark makeup around eyes adds that "dead for 1,000 years" look.

With enough stitches, this costume can be taken on and off without self-destructing.

● HIPPIE
(For '60s Day.)

Child wears faded blue jeans (rips in knees are great). Sew colorful patches here and there. Girls can wear jeans or a long, flowing India-print skirt or dress. Either a T-shirt, India-print shirt, turtleneck, or plain shirt is fine, and a vest is a nice touch (if one is available). Child wears sandals, work boots, or sneakers.

"Love beads" (see **Flower Bead Necklace,** page 127) are fun to make and are the perfect "hippie jewelry." Child can also make paper Peace Sign buttons (see illustration). Attach to shirt with loop of tape.

Part child's hair down the middle and tie a headband or bandana around head.

Face painting is fun and looks great: flowers, peace signs, rainbows. Girls wear long, dangly earrings.

▲ **DALMATIAN**

Child wears white sweatsuit, white shirt and pants, white leotard and tights, or some combination of the above. Cut dots out of black felt. Dots can be anywhere from 1 inch to 2 inches across. Use *water-soluble* white glue to attach black dots to white outfit. (This glue *washes out.*)

Use white and black makeup to add spots to child's face.

Or

Use white fabric to make Dalmatian cap and tail, as shown in illustration. Attach tail with safety pin.

Child can make "dog tags" out of stiff paper, if desired, and wear around neck on a string.

When costume is no longer needed, peel black dots off clothes. Launder as usual and glue residue will wash right out.

Optional Cap and Tail

cut 2

cut 4

3" elastic

■ FLOWER

You need: Poster board, approximately 24 inches square
Poster paints
Scissors
Markers
Ribbon or string
Popsicle sticks (optional)

Child does: Decides what color flower will be. Decides how many petals the flower should have.

You and   (See illustration.)
child do: Cut hole in center of poster board square, so that child's face fits comfortably in hole. The fit should be snug, but *not* too tight!
Draw the desired flower shape around the hole, following child's instructions as to number and shape of petals. Petal cutting lines should end at least 2 inches from hole.

Child does: Cuts out flower along cutting lines. (Save poster board scraps.)
Paints petals desired color(s). Paint *both sides* of flower, allowing first side to dry before flipping poster board over.

You and   Follow directions for **How to Make a Mask Stay on**
child do: **Your Head** page 169.
If petals are too floppy, reinforce back of flower with Popsicle sticks taped across weak points.

back of flower mask

156

Child does: Uses poster board scraps to make "leaves," if desired. Use paints or markers to color them green.

Child wears green or brown clothes, as "stem." Leaves can be taped or safety-pinned to clothes.

● LUMBERJACK/PAUL BUNYAN

Child wears plaid shirt, jeans, and boots or sneakers. Suspenders add a nice touch. Tuck jeans into boots. Make an axe out of cardboard. (You may want to use a double layer of cardboard, glued or taped together.) Cover axe blade with aluminum foil and secure with clear tape. Color axe handle brown or black, or wrap with masking tape or dark vinyl tape.

● BACKWARDS BOY/BACKWARDS GIRL
(A simple, fast, and funny costume.)

Child wears all clothes backwards. Try to include a backwards hat. Make or buy a mask and wear on *back* of head. If trick-or-treating, child can walk backwards (guided by a friend or adult), extending trick-or-treat bag behind him/her.

● POLITICIAN

Child wears dress clothes (boys should wear a tie; girls wear a conservative skirt and blouse). Wears oversized "Vote for <u>Child's Name</u>" button.

Hands out "Vote for <u>Child's Name</u>" fliers, stating platform. (See example.) If copy machine is available, fliers can even feature child's photograph.

■ MALE COLONIST/GEORGE WASHINGTON

Child wears **Quick Knickers** (page 173) with knee socks, **George Washington Wig** (page 173), white shirt or blouse, a vest (if one is available), and can tape paper cutout **Buckles** to shoes (page 172).

■ FEMALE COLONIST

Child wears long, dark skirt with white **Apron** (page 170) over it. White blouse. Kerchief in hair. Shawl.

158

CARDBOARD BOX COSTUMES

Cardboard boxes can be covered with freezer paper, pieces of blank newsprint, brown paper bags, or prepasted wallpaper samples, to make unusual and creative costumes. Cardboard also takes paint and spray paint very well.

! Please be aware, however, that cardboard box costumes can be bulky and awkward. While he or she is wearing this costume, keep your child away from stairs!

■ CANDY MACHINE
(This is a big hit at Halloween parties.)

You need: Large cardboard box
Paper or paint to cover box
Markers or poster paints
Scissors or sharp knife
Masking or strapping tape
Bag of inexpensive candy

You do: (See illustration.)
Remove top flaps of box. Turn box bottom side up.
Cut hole for child's head in bottom of box. Box will rest on child's shoulders. Make sure child can walk easily with head sticking out of box.

You and child do: Using either paper or paint, cover entire surface of box. If using paint, allow paint to dry thoroughly before proceeding.

You do: With child standing in box, figure out and mark appropriate spot for "Candy Dispenser Slot." It should be

159

within child's easy reach from inside the box.

With child *out* of box, cut Dispenser Slot. This should be about 3 × 5 inches for easy dispensing.

If child wants, you can also cut a money slot.

Child does: Decorates outside of box to look like a candy machine. (See illustration.) This can be done using poster paints, markers, or making paper signs and attaching them to box with glue or tape. Be sure to add labels, directions, and arrows so people will know how to "operate" machine.

At time of party, child stands inside box, equipped with bag of inexpensive candy. When children insert a penny (or homemade paper coin), child drops piece of candy out Dispenser Slot.

! *Note of Caution:* Because this costume is cumbersome, it is appropriate for indoor use only. KEEP CHILD AWAY FROM STAIRS.

DINNER TABLE

You need: Large square box
Sharp scissors or knife
Masking tape or strapping tape
Any large, blank paper (Freezer paper works well.)
  Or Inexpensive paper tablecloth
2–4 paper plates
2–4 settings of plastic flatware (knives, forks, spoons)
2–4 paper napkins
2–4 paper or plastic cups
White glue
Markers or poster paint

You and   (See illustration.)
child do: Remove top flaps from box.
Turn box over and cover bottom and sides of box with
    blank paper. Decorate it to look like a tablecloth (fringe,
    checkered pattern, lace trim, or plain). *Or* use an
    inexpensive paper tablecloth.
Cut hole in center of box bottom for child's head to fit
    through. Box will rest on child's shoulders. If box is
    smallish, you may want to cut armholes.
Glue on place settings, cups, and napkins. Add a teapot or
    sugar bowl from a plastic tea set, if desired.
For a final touch, child can wear a real or paper lamp
    shade on his/her head.

!*Note of*   Because this costume is cumbersome, it is appropriate for
!*Caution:*   indoor use only. KEEP CHILD AWAY FROM STAIRS.

■ JUICE BOX

You need: Medium-size cardboard box
Paper or paint to cover box
Markers or poster paints
Cardboard tube from paper towels or gift wrap
Scissors or sharp knife

You do: (See illustration.)
Remove top flaps of box. Turn box bottom side up.
Cut hole for child's head in bottom of box. Box will rest on child's shoulders. Make sure child can walk easily with head sticking out of box.
Cut armholes in sides of box.

You and
child do: Using either paper or paint, cover entire surface of box. If using paint, allow paint to dry thoroughly before proceeding.
Copy packaging of child's favorite boxed drink.
Cut a hole, the diameter of the cardboard tube, in the top of juice box near a corner. Insert tube and secure with tape on inside of box. Tube is juice box "straw."

!Note of
!Caution: Because this costume is cumbersome, it is appropriate for indoor use only. KEEP CHILD AWAY FROM STAIRS.

162

■ TELEVISION SET

You need: Medium-to-large cardboard box
Brown paper or paint to cover box
Heavy tape
Plastic bottle caps
2 drinking straws
Heavy scissors or sharp knife
Aluminum foil or construction paper
Markers
Glue or clear tape

You do: (See illustration.)
Cut top flaps off box. Turn box bottom side up.
Cut a television screen shape out of one side of the box.
   Box will rest on child's head.
Depending on size of box, you may want to cut armholes.

You and child do: Cover box with brown paper or paint to give it a "wood" finish. *Or* cover box with aluminum foil for a futuristic look. (This is highly visible when trick-or-treating in the dark.)

Cover plastic bottle caps with aluminum foil or construction paper and attach to television with tape or glue. Label these knobs: On, Off, Channels, etc.

Use heavy tape to attach straws to top of television in "rabbit ears" position.

Idea: This television can be made with a small-to-medium box that fits over child's head and shoulders.

!*Note of Caution:* Because this costume is cumbersome, it is appropriate for indoor use only. KEEP CHILD AWAY FROM STAIRS.

■ ## GIFT BOX

You need: Medium-size cardboard box
Gift wrap or plain white paper
Construction paper (1 color)
Big gift-wrap bow
Tape
Scissors
Heavy scissors or sharp knife

You do: Cut top flaps off box.
Turn box bottom side up.
Cut hole in bottom of box for child's head. Cut holes in sides of box for child's arms.

You and child do: Cover box with gift wrap.
Tape construction paper strips (3 inches wide) around box to resemble ribbon.
Child wears big gift-wrap ribbon on head.

!*Note of Caution:* Because this costume is cumbersome, it is appropriate for indoor use only. KEEP CHILD AWAY FROM STAIRS.

SANDWICH BOARD COSTUMES

■ TUBE OF TOOTHPASTE

You need: 2 pieces of white poster board, approximately 15 inches
wide and 28 inches long
Pencil
Ruler
Markers or poster paints
Ribbon or string
2 pieces stiff, white paper
Clear tape

You and (See illustration, page 167.)
child do: Use pencil to draw facsimile of front and back of toothpaste tube on separate pieces of poster board. Use ruler
when necessary.
Color drawing with markers and/or poster paints.
Punch holes in top of poster board pieces and attach
ribbon to create a sandwich board for child.

To make (See illustration.)
cap: Make a cap for your tube of toothpaste by taping two
pieces of white paper together so that they measure
approximately 8½ × 21½ inches.
Bring ends together and tape so cap fits child's head and
is slightly cone shaped. Trim any uneven ends.
Use a black marker or black poster paint to draw vertical
lines on the cap.
Secure cap with bobby pins.

■ **M & M**

You need: 2 poster board or cardboard circles approximately 2–3 feet in diameter
Paint and brushes
M & M's wrapper (for model)
Ribbon or string

Child does: Decides on color of costume. (Availability of colored poster board or paint may influence this decision!)

You and child do: (See illustration.)
If necessary, paint both circles of poster board or cardboard. Allow to dry.
Using M & M's wrapper as model, carefully copy "M" in center of each circle.
Paint "M" white.
Punch 2 holes in top of circles, about 7–9 inches apart.
Attach ribbon to create sandwich board for child.

Idea: Child may also want to wear clothes and cap of matching color.

● **MOVABLE MASTERPIECE**

You need: Square of cardboard or poster board, 2–3 feet across.
Poster paints *and/or* collage materials and glue
Wide vinyl tape or duct tape
Scissors
Ribbon or string

Child does: (See illustration.)
Creates his/her own version of an artistic masterpiece. This can be a self-portrait, abstract art, a multimedia collage of paints, pasta, and magazine pictures, or whatever.
Frames artwork with wide strips of vinyl tape or construction paper.
Labels masterpiece with title and artist.

You and child do: Punch 2 holes in top of frame, centered and about 12 inches apart. Attach about 20 inches of ribbon and hang around child's neck.

■ BOARD GAME

(Child dresses as favorite board game.)

You need: 2 pieces of poster board
Markers
Construction paper, aluminum foil, etc.
Glue
Ribbon or string

You and
child do: Draw a facsimile of the board game *box cover* on one piece of poster board. Try to be as accurate as possible.

On the second piece of poster board, draw the game board itself. If this is too difficult, draw a simplified version of the board. Color it in, trying to match colors to the board.

Use aluminum foil to make models of any metallic game pieces and glue them to the game board.

Use construction paper, cardboard, or other materials to make flat or three-dimensional game pieces, cards, tokens, etc. Glue to board. (You can also use one or two pieces of actual game money if this is at a surplus. Glue these to the game board too.) You can buy inexpensive dice and glue them to the board.

Punch holes in top of poster board pieces and attach ribbon, to create a sandwich board for child. "Cover" of game goes in front.

ACCESSORIES

● **SILVER BEAD NECKLACE**

You need: Aluminum foil
             Needle and thread long enough to go over your head

Child does: Tears foil into many pieces, each about 1½-inch square.
               Forms pieces into balls about ⅜ inch in diameter. *Do not*
                 compact foil, or the needle won't poke through.
               Threads foil balls to make necklace.

Note: This is a handy trick for a last-minute gypsy costume.

HOW TO MAKE A MASK STAY ON YOUR HEAD

(To avoid that annoying ''slip-down'' problem, use string and heavy tape to make a mask more secure.)

You need: Mask (homemade or store-bought)
18-inch piece of string
10-inch piece of string
Heavy tape (Vinyl or duct tape works well.)
Scissors

You and child do: (See illustration.)
Turn finished mask face down.
Tape one end of the 18-inch piece of string to one side of mask next to an eye hole.
Tape one end of the 10-inch piece of string to the top center of the mask.
With child wearing mask, bring 18-inch string behind child's head and tape to other side of mask next to eye hole so that mask fits snugly but comfortably.
While child holds mask in position, bring 10-inch string over top of child's head and tie the loose end to the longer piece of string, as shown.
Trim ends of string.

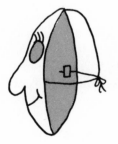

back view

▲ CAPE OR APRON

(For superhero, vampire, Zorro, royalty, etc.)

You need: About 1 yard of fabric 36–45 inches wide (Fabric store remnant piles are a great place to find potential capes. Shiny, slinky fabrics are especially fun for children to swirl around in.)

Needle and thread

Iron (Optional, but makes sewing easier.)

You do: (See illustration, pages 171 and 172.)

Use bias edges of fabric as sides of cape, to avoid having to hem sides.

If necessary, cut fabric to desired cape size (rectangle or square).

Cut a 3-inch strip of fabric from the top edge of cape to form neckband. (1)

Fold edges of strip over ⅜ inch and iron. (2)

Fold strip in half the long way and iron. (3)

Hem bottom edge of cape. (Sewing can be done by hand or by machine.)

Use running stitch to baste along top edge of cape. (4)

Gather cape to width that matches child's shoulders (approximately 12–16 inches). (5)

Center gathered edge of cape inside folded neckband strip. Pin in place, and sew as shown. (6)

Ideas: Other ways of attaching cape to child: (See illustrations.)

● Follow steps 1–6 above, but use a shorter fabric strip, so that strip overlaps 1–2 inches around child's neck. Sew Velcro tabs to ends of strip for Velcro closure. (7)

● *If cape will be worn over sweatshirt,* hem top and bottom edges of cape. Baste and gather only the outer thirds of the top edge. (8)

Use overhand stitch to attach these gathered sections to sweatshirt shoulders, leaving center section loose and sagging slightly. (9)

Note: Child may want to trim back of cape with appropriate symbol. Have child draw a paper pattern of the desired symbol (Batman, lightning bolt, royal crest, etc.). Cut design out of felt and sew on or attach with water-soluble white glue.

- *Apron Variation*

This same idea can be used to make a quick apron for a woman in Colonial times. Use white cloth. Adjust the apron length and width to suit the child, and make the ties long enough to go around child's waist.

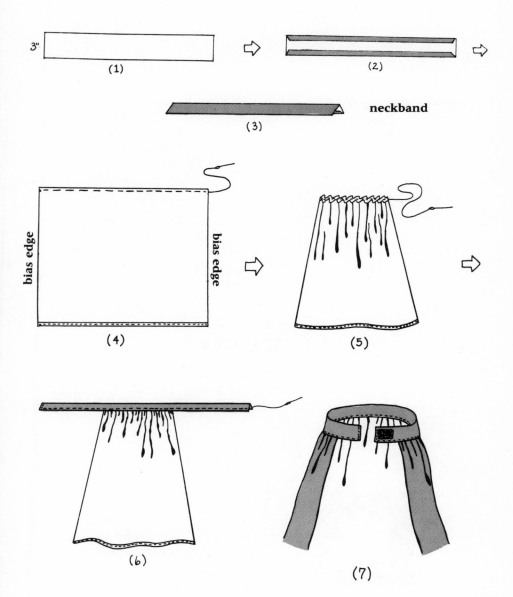

3"

(1)

(2)

(3) **neckband**

bias edge

bias edge

(4)

(5)

(6)

(7)

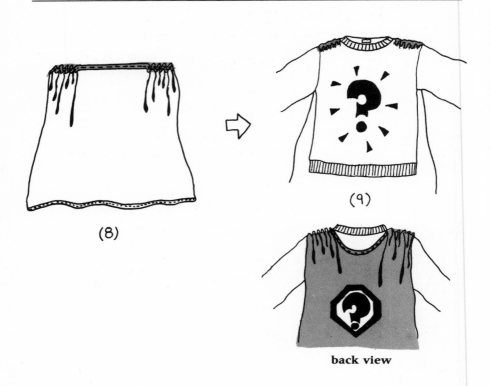

(8)

(9)

back view

● COLONIAL SHOE BUCKLES

(See illustration.) Cut two 2–3-inch squares of black construction paper. Fold squares in half and cut out inside, leaving ½-inch border. Tape to top of shoes.

QUICK KNICKERS

(For Pilgrim costume, Colonial times, etc.)

You need: Pair of old sweatpants (gray, black, or blue are best)
Scissors
Velcro (or 2 safety pins)
Needle and thread

You and child do: Cut pants to 2 inches below child's knees.
Sew Velcro tabs so that pants are snug below knee.

Or

Safety-pin fabric after knickers are on.

GEORGE WASHINGTON WIG

You need: Swim cap
6 × 1-inch piece of scrap fabric, ribbon, or felt
12-inch black ribbon
Rubber cement
Cotton balls
Stapler

You and child do: (See illustration.)
Staple strip of fabric to bottom of swim cap in back.
Use rubber cement to cover outside of swim cap with cotton balls. Glue cotton balls to both sides of fabric strip to form "ponytail."
Let dry. Have child try on wig and add cotton balls to "bald spots."
Tie black ribbon around ponytail, 1 inch from end, to form a bow.

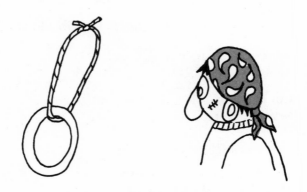

● PIRATE OR GYPSY EARRING

Cut small hoop shape out of white poster board and color gold or bright yellow. Tie a loop of yarn through hoop and adjust so yarn fits comfortably around child's entire ear. Cover that ear with kerchief, allowing only earring to show. (See illustration.)

● PIRATE OR GYPSY KERCHIEF

Fold square bandana or scarf on the diagonal. Tie ends at back of child's neck. Kerchief can cover one or both ears, depending on look desired, or it can rest farther back on head, secured with bobby pins.

● BELT

A very quick and shiny belt can be made from a long piece of aluminum foil folded to about 2 inches wide. Wrap around child's waist, trim excess, and tape inside and out with heavy tape.

● GLOVES

Depending on the color and style needed, child might use winter gloves. Or try inexpensive rubber kitchen gloves. These usually come in bright yellow or orange. You can trim the cuffs with scissors, and draw details on them with permanent marker.

OUTDOOR PROJECTS AND ACTIVITIES

Bird feeders are quick and inexpensive projects with lasting results. After a few days, birds will discover and flock to your feeder. Have a bird identification book handy!

Try to hang these feeders where squirrels can't get at them (unless you like squirrels). If you hang your bird feeder on a tree, use a long string looped over a branch and secured to the trunk or lower branch (as shown in Figure 6 of **Soda Bottle Bird Feeder,** page 178). This way, you can easily lower the feeder to refill it.

Bird feeders are an easy and worthwhile group project for scout meetings or parties, with a nice take-home result.

PINE CONE BIRD FEEDER

You need:	Large pine cone (Try to find one at least 5 inches long, with large, open scales.)
	Long piece of string
	¼ cup peanut butter (approximately)
	⅛ cup cornmeal (approximately)
	Small bowl
	Butter knife

You and child do: (See illustration.)
Pine cone bird feeder will hang stem down. Tie one end of string to pine cone scales, as shown.
Combine peanut butter and cornmeal in bowl.

Child does: Using the butter knife, child spreads peanut butter mixture on pine cone scales.

You and child do: Hang bird feeder in the shade.

Note: If weather is hot, use a bit more cornmeal.

Ideas: Try different peanut butter mixes on future pine cones:
- ¼ cup peanut butter and ⅛ cup bird seed mix
- equal parts peanut butter and suet, melted and mixed with bird seed. Apply to pine cone when cooled.

■ SODA BOTTLE BIRD FEEDER

You need: Plastic soda bottle with cap (16-ounce size is nice)
Permanent marker
Sharp knife
Sharp scissors
Strong string: two 12-inch lengths and one very long piece
Paper towel
Bird seed

Child does: (See illustration.)
Peels label off bottle.
Rinses bottle with water.
Using permanent marker, draws the outline of the openings to be cut out. The bottom of the openings should be 2 inches up from the bottom of the bottle. The openings should be about 2 inches tall, 2 inches wide, and on opposite sides of the bottle. (1)

You do: Use sharp knife to start a cut along each of the cutting
!   lines.

Child does: Using scissors, child continues to cut along cutting lines. (2) The plastic edges are a little sharp, but they won't hurt the birds.
Dries the inside of the bottle with a paper towel.

You and   Tie one 12-inch length of string around the top of the
child do: bottle, as shown in Figure 3. Use three or four overhand knots, to make it really secure.
Tie the other 12-inch length of string around the top of the bottle. There should be a knot on either side of the bottle top. (4)
Take the longest string from each side and tie them together as shown in Figure 5. This will make a loop of string at the top of the bottle. Attach the long piece of string to this loop, fill the feeder with bird seed, and hang your bird feeder. (6)

Optional: You can add a perch to your bird feeder by punching holes about ½ inch down from the openings and sliding a stick through the bottle.

178

(1)

(2)

(3)

(4)

(5)

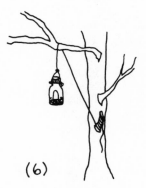

(6)

MILK CARTON BIRD FEEDER

You need: Cardboard milk or juice carton (half-gallon size)
Masking tape
Permanent marker or ballpoint pen
Ruler
Screwdriver or awl (to punch hole in top of carton)
Scissors
Paper towel
String
Bird seed

Child does: (See illustration.)
Washes out carton.
Tapes top of carton closed. (1)
Draws 2 × 3-inch rectangles on two (or four) sides of carton. Bottom of rectangles should be about 2 inches from bottom of carton. (2)

You do: Punch two holes in top of carton, as shown. (3)
Using either screwdriver or scissors, *start* cutting on rectangular cutting lines.
Do not cut along *top* of rectangle!

Child does: Continues to cut along all side and bottom cutting lines, *leaving tops of rectangles uncut.* (4) If any tears or stray cuts occur, mend with masking tape.
Measures about 1–1½ inches from top line and cuts across to form a flap. Bends flaps up to form an awning over openings. (5)
Dries inside of carton with paper towel.
Threads one end of string through holes in top of carton.

You and child do: Tie strong knot in string to hold feeder securely.
Fill feeder with seed.
Hang feeder.

Optional: If desired, you can punch holes near bottom of carton and slide one or two sticks through as perches. Then add seed and hang feeder.

Note: *Any* size carton can be used. Simply adjust the size of the openings accordingly.

(1)

(2)

(3)

(4)

(5)

■ SPONGE PRINTS

You need: Collection of leaves 2 inches across or larger (Small-leafed plants such as ferns do not work well.)
Poster paints
Paint brush
Piece of sponge 1 inch across
Paper (white or construction)

You and child do: (See illustrations, pages 182 and 183.)
Place one leaf on paper.
Use paint brush to apply paint to end of damp sponge piece.
Hold leaf in place with one hand as child uses sponge to gently dab paint around edges of leaf. Reapply paint if necessary. Change colors, if desired, rinsing sponge and brush in water.
When leaf edges, stem, and surrounding area are painted, carefully lift leaf to reveal print.

Idea: Sponge Prints make nice **Note Cards,** page 60.

■ NATURE PRINTS

You need: Collection of leaves (also try ferns, clover, feathers, twigs, certain flower petals)
Poster paints
Soft paint brush
Paper (white or construction)
Scrap paper (not newspaper)

You and
child do: (See illustration.)

Work with one leaf at a time.

Gently paint the most textured side of leaf. Paint should cover entire leaf, but should not be too thick. Experiment a few times to determine proper amount of paint for printing.

Lay leaf, paint side down, on paper.

Cover with one sheet of scrap paper, and gently press leaf with fingers.

Remove scrap paper and carefully peel leaf up to reveal print.

If print is too light, use more paint next time.

If print is too dark and the leaf texture doesn't show, continue to print with that leaf, using up excess paint. Use less paint next time.

Ideas: Paint nature objects one solid color, or use two or more colors to create a jeweled effect. When leaves are painted with random splotches of green, red, and yellow, the print looks like autumn foliage!

Nature Prints make nice **Note Cards,** page 60.

■ ## NATURE BOOKMARK
(These make great souvenirs or gifts after a trip!)

You need: Construction paper or plain white paper
Markers or crayons
Clear Con-Tact paper
Flat nature objects (small leaves, dry petals, ferns, small flowers, etc.)
Scissors
9 inches of ribbon or yarn (optional)

Child does: Collects nature objects.

You and child do: (See example.)
Cut paper 6 inches long and 1½–2 inches wide.
If desired, child can write his/her name, the name of bookmark recipient, or the place where nature objects were found at the bottom of the paper.
Lay paper, writing side up, on sticky side of Con-Tact paper.
Arrange nature objects on paper and cover with a second sheet of Con-Tact paper. Trim Con-Tact paper, leaving a ¼-inch border around paper.

Ideas: Lay a loop of ribbon or yarn at the top of the bookmark before covering with the second sheet of Con-Tact paper.
Omit the paper and arrange nature objects directly on strips of Con-Tact paper to create a transparent bookmark. Use a larger piece of Con-Tact paper (6 × 6 inches) to create a transparent Nature Windowhanging.

NATURE BOOKMARK

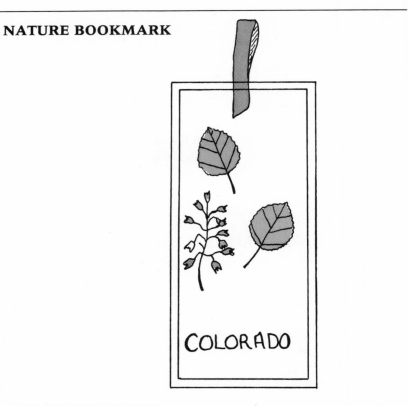

SEASON PLACEMAT

186

● SEASON PLACEMATS

You need: Construction paper
Clear Con-Tact paper
Scissors
Seasonal flat objects or creations (see *Ideas*, below)

Child does: Arranges desired objects on construction paper. Objects can be combined with a drawing, if desired, to make a multimedia placemat (see *Ideas*).

You and child do: Cover both sides with clear Con-Tact paper.

Ideas: *Spring*—paper cutouts of flowers, petals, buds, etc. Drawings of sun, rainbows, blue sky. Magazine pictures of flowers, baby animals, etc. Feature lots of pastels. A temporary placemat can feature real flower petals pressed under Con-Tact paper, but the petal colors will last only a couple of days. *Or* placemats can have a sports motif, featuring drawings or pictures of baseball, soccer, etc.

Summer—drawings or rubbings of seashells. Paper cutouts of sailboats on a crayon ocean. Magazine pictures of fish, summer sports, camping, hiking, mountains, desert, etc. Brochures of summer destinations can result in "family trip" placemats, featuring favorite places visited during vacation.

Autumn—colorful leaves against a contrasting background. Sports motif could feature pictures of football players. Or school theme could be featured with drawings of chalkboards, math problems, alphabet, friends' names, etc.

Winter—white paper snowman and snowflake cutouts against a dark or black background. Collage made up of colorful bits of gift wrap and ribbon. Drawings of skiing, skating, sledding, hockey, etc.

SIDEWALK GAMES

(Invent new and different "hopscotch-type" games.)

You need: Chalk (Try to find colored chalk. It makes the games more attractive and can be used for sidewalk art as well.)
Smooth sidewalk, driveway, playground, etc.

Sidewalk Game #1

(See example.) Use chalk to draw a long line of circles, squares, triangles, etc., each about 12–18 inches across. A different action must be performed while standing in each shape. For instance, spin around three times inside circles, run in place while reciting the alphabet inside squares, do ten jumping jacks inside triangles, etc.

Players jump from space to space. A group of children can play this game simultaneously, giving each other a 1 minute headstart.

Or

Kids can play individually, just for fun, or to see who can complete all activities in the shortest amount of time.

Sidewalk Game #2

(See example.) This game is a little like traditional hopscotch, but trickier. You may want to plot the game board pattern on paper before drawing it on a big scale.

Once again, each shape calls for a different action. Players play individually, throwing markers into the numbered spaces as they progress through the game. For instance, in the pictured Game #2, the first player would toss his/her marker into space #1 and have to invent a new dance step. The second player would then do the same.

Player #1 would then throw his/her marker into space #2, do a new dance step in space #1, hop to space #2, and do ten jumping jacks. Play would continue until one or all players finished the board.

Sidewalk Game #3

This game uses either of the above patterns but the actions require the use of a *ball*. Children can decide on actions depending on what kind of ball is available. For instance:

Squares: Bounce the ball on the ground ten times.

Circles: Toss the ball in the air and clap before catching it, ten times.

Triangles: Dribble the ball through your legs once.

Sidewalk Art

Smooth pavement of any size is a potential canvas for the sidewalk artist! Use colored chalk to draw tiny masterpieces on a flagstone walk. Or gather friends to make a driveway-size mural.

Children can leave artwork until the next rain, or he/she may want to blast the picture with a hose.

SIDEWALK GAME #1

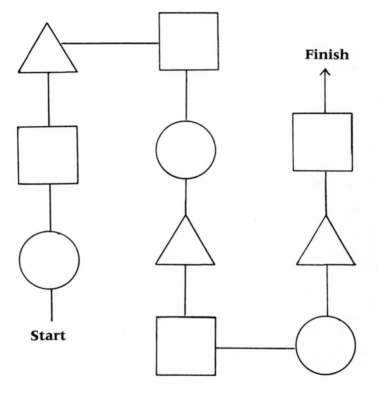

Finish

Start

KEY

○   **Spin around 3 times**

▢   **Run in place while reciting the alphabet**

△   **Do 10 jumping jacks**

SIDEWALK GAME #2

Finish

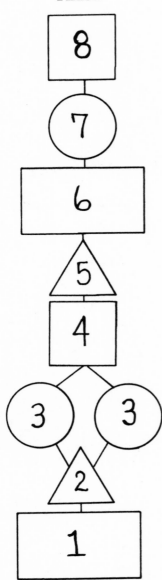

Start

KEY

  Invent a crazy
new dance step

△ Do 10 jumping jacks

○ Touch head, shoulders,
knees, toes, 8 times

☐ Run around the
game board

SIMPLE POTPOURRI

You need: Petals from a collection of fragrant flowers
Sunny windowsill
Perfume (optional)

Child does: Collects petals. After making potpourri a number of times, child will learn which local flowers work best, have the nicest scent when dry, etc.

Child spreads petals in a sunny, dry spot protected from wind. Leave to dry for a few days. Petals must be *completely dry* or potpourri will mold. Petals will shrivel and curl, but will retain their color and fragrance.

When petals are dry, add a drop or two of perfume, if desired.

Store potpourri in small bowl or use it to make **Sachets,** page 111.

POCKET BUBBLER

You need: Undiluted dish detergent
Plastic drinking straw (Must be *dry.*)
Small cup or bowl (Must be *dry.*)

Child does: Pours a small amount of detergent into bowl.

Dips one end of straw into detergent.

Aims away from people and blows a long stream of tiny bubbles!

Slower blowing results in larger bubbles.

Note: If Pocket Bubbler doesn't work, start again, making sure that straw and cup are dry, and that dish detergent is completely undiluted! Try not to get dish detergent too foamy.

! This activity is *not* appropriate for very young children who might suck detergent through the straw.

HELIUM BALLOON MESSAGE

(The next time your child has a helium balloon, perhaps he/she would like to send a message.)

You need: Helium balloon
Postal service post card (with postage attached)
Ballpoint pen

You and child do: First, determine whether balloon will carry a post card. (Old helium balloons may be too weak.)
Put child's name and address on front of post card.
On back of post card, write the following:

My name is _____. I am _____ years old. I released this balloon on [date].

Please write your name, where you found this balloon, and the date you found it in the space below. Then drop this card in a mail box.

Thank you!

Punch a hole in postcard, attach to balloon string, and release on a breezy day.

Note: Be *absolutely sure* your child understands that the helium balloon will be released and will sail *away*.

CREATURE COUNT

A Creature Count is a time for you and your child to get comfortable outdoors, sit quietly, listen, and watch for as many "creatures" as you can.

You need: Paper and pencil
Watch or timer

You and child do: Let your child decide on the location and duration of your Creature Count. A young child may be able to sit for only 5 minutes; an older child may sit for 20 minutes or more.

Try different locations on different days: middle of yard, forest, playground, field, seashore, sidewalk, near a creek or river, a mountaintop, etc.

Watch and listen carefully. In the allotted amount of time, see how many creatures you and your child can see or hear. List them on your paper, along with the date, time of day, and amount of time you sat.

Keep track of your Creature Counts to compare and discover the best time and location for creature watching.

Common creatures to watch for: ants, spiders, flies, mosquitoes, butterflies, moths, dragonflies, beetles, grasshoppers, crickets, worms, caterpillars, minnows, tadpoles, frogs, toads, snakes, mice, chipmunks, squirrels, many different kinds of birds, cats, dogs, cows, horses, sheep, goats

Creatures you might see if you're lucky: fish, turtles, lizards, salamanders, deer, foxes, woodchucks, raccoons, skunks, eagles, hawks, herons, seals, etc.

Creatures you might hear, but not see: crickets, frogs, birds, coyotes, etc.

● ■ ▲   **BACKYARD EXERCISE COURSE**

You need: Simple map of backyard, park, play field

Or

Numbered sheets of paper to be posted at various spots in the yard

Any necessary exercise equipment (jump ropes, balls, etc.)

You and   (See illustration.)

child do: Choose different locations in yard and number them on the map as Station #1, Station #2, etc.

Child decides what exercise should be done at each station.

Briefly describe each exercise on map, as shown. Station #1 should be the time to *stretch,* to avoid pulled muscles!

Or

Post numbered sheets of paper, with exercise instructions, at various locations throughout yard. These signs should also point the way to the next station.

Whole   Family and friends can follow map or directions, doing

family does: various exercises from station to station.

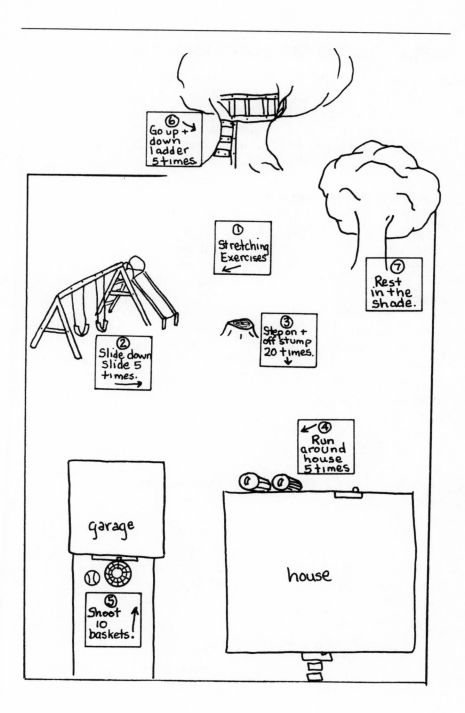

●■▲ BACKYARD SCAVENGER HUNTS

This is an easy and fun game for one child or a group of children. Children can cooperate to find all the items on the list, or they can compete to find the most items. Sample lists are below, but you should adjust your list to correspond with your own backyard and the ages of your children. Decide ahead of time whether children should collect items or simply check them off on their lists.

Scavenger Hunt Examples:

Spring
dandelions
leaf bud
spider web
flower petal
robin
baseball or bat
gardening tool
sprouting plant
chipmunk or squirrel
butterfly or moth

Summer
pink flower petal
Y-shaped twig
furry animal
toy
something plastic
insect
something orange
ball
garden hose
three-leaf clover

Fall
red leaf
acorn
football
rake
pumpkin
yellow leaf
bicycle
big stick
bird feeder
pine cone

Winter
sled
icicle
mitten or glove
snowman
twig
snow shovel
ski pole
brown leaf
snow angel
hat with pom-pom

■ SNOW SCULPTURE

Instead of the traditional snowman, try sculpting unusual shapes out of snow. Start with a big pile of packed snow (at the side of a shoveled driveway, for instance). Decide on a figure and start carving away and adding on to get the features you want. Create huge faces, animals (try a whale, octopus, or snow snake for starters), or a snow house. Use icicles for teeth or trim, and accent features with diluted food coloring in a spray bottle.

● FLASHLIGHT WALK

If you live in a rural or suburban area, give everyone a flashlight and go for a night walk. Very young children may feel most comfortable walking near their own house, peeking into brightly lit and familiar rooms from the dark outdoors.

! Older children will want to venture farther into the night. Either way, *close adult supervision is a must!*

After the initial excitement of flashlights and darkness wears off, encourage child/children to listen and look around. Watch and listen for night creatures: fireflies, crickets, glow worms, owls. Compare night noises to day noises. Depending on the season, your night walk may be very noisy (summer) or very silent (winter).

Then go home for a cool drink or some hot cocoa.

● STAR GAZING

You don't need a fancy telescope to enjoy the night sky. In fact, a telescope is often more frustrating than not for a young child. On a moonless night, far from city lights, the naked eye can see as many as 4,000 stars. With standard 7 × 50 binoculars, more than 50,000 stars become visible.

Look for the Milky Way and common constellations. Your newspaper may have a weekly column describing which constellations and planets are most obvious in the night sky. The library is a good place to find a star chart, to identify which constellations are visible in each season.

Wait for a full moon on a clear night and use binoculars to get a wonderfully detailed view of its surface.

TREASURE HUNTS

You don't need a fancy treasure to have a great treasure hunt. The real fun is in the hunting. Treasures can be a snack (healthy or sweet), a small gift, a note ("You found it!"), a penny, etc. Party guests can hunt for their favor bags.

Here are a number of different treasure hunts, ranging from very easy to more challenging. They may be set up indoors, outdoors, or both.

● FOLLOW THE ARROWS

Paper arrows are taped to walls, furniture, stairways, and floor. Outdoors, attach arrows to trees, playground equipment, rocks, etc. Players follow the arrows in a long, involved maze to get to the treasure. Arrows may be *numbered* to eliminate any confusion.

This treasure hunt is an easy one for a child to set up unassisted.

● FOLLOW THE STRING

The length of the string controls the length of the hunt. Secure one end of a ball of string to the treasure and hide the treasure. Then unroll the string as you wander through the house (or backyard), weaving under, over, around, and through fun places for your child to crawl.

Give child what's left of the ball of string with instructions to "Follow the string, winding it up as you go."

Note: Young children may find it easier to wind the string around a piece of cardboard.

If more than one child is hunting, children may work as a team to follow one string. Or use colored yarn and make a number of different hunts, ending in different places. Each child gets his/her own color to follow.

● *X* MARKS THE SPOT

(See illustration.) Make a map of the area where the treasure will be hidden. This can be done by an adult, a child, or as a group effort.

Adult hides treasure, and marks an *X* on the map. Child/children must read the map to find the treasure. Treasure can be hidden again, in a new spot, with a new *X* on the map. Or *child* can hide treasure and draw *X* on map.

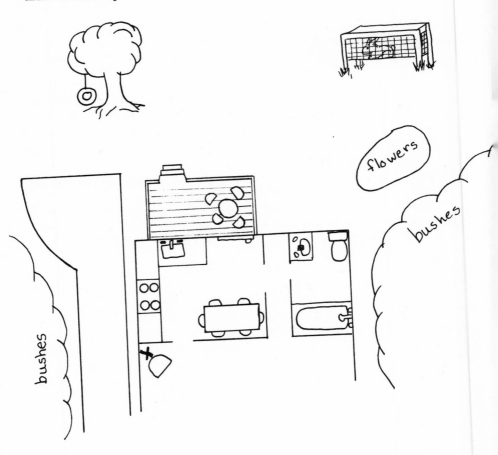

■ ▲   BACKYARD ORIENTEERING TREASURE HUNT

You need: Compass
Yardstick or tape measure
Paper and pencil
Treasure (Can be anything: penny, small candy, ribbon tied to tree, any kind of marker.)

You do: Show child how to use compass to find directions.
Prepare list of instructions for child to follow:
Example:
1. Start at our front door.
2. Walk south 20 feet.
3. Walk west until you get to a tree.
4. Walk south 6 feet.
5. Walk east 3 feet.
6. Walk south 20 feet.
7. Walk west to a pine tree.
8. Walk north about 10 feet and look for a gray rock. The treasure is on the rock!

You and child do: Child may need/want your help and guidance for early excursions. (Using a compass is tricky at first.) As child's skills improve, orienteering instructions can get more complicated, using NW, SW, SE, SW, and longer distances.
Child may want to write orienteering directions for *you.*

Variation: If a directional compass isn't available, this activity may be done using a simple map of the yard showing landmarks and directions. (See **Maps,** page 145.)

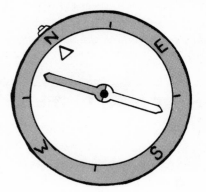

■ CLUE TO CLUE

Write and hide a series of clues on scraps of paper, leading child/children from one clue to the next. The clues can be straightforward ("Look on the table") or more difficult ("You watch me but I don't watch you," indicating the television set). Picture clues can be used for children who are not yet reading.

Example:

Give child clue #1 which says, "Look under your pillow."

Child looks under pillow and finds clue #2 which says, "Look under the rock on the front steps."

Child looks under rock and finds clue #3 which says, "Look behind the blue sofa."

Etc.

The more clues, the longer the hunt. Try to lead child in and out of rooms, up and down stairs, or from front yard to backyard. This makes the hunt more exciting and makes it last longer.

■ CLUE TO MAP TO CLUE TO MAP

Save maps and clues from previous hunts. Alternate maps and clues so that some maps lead to clues and some clues lead to maps.

▲ NEIGHBORHOOD HUNT

This treasure hunt for older children involves the cooperation of other people or households, and lots of planning ahead.

Children walk or ride bicycles from house to house, apartment to apartment, or even business to business. They must say a prearranged "code word" and will then receive a clue and/or instructions for their next destination. *An adult should accompany the group on their hunt.*

● TREASURE HUNT IN THE SNOW

Fill a spray bottle with a strong mixture of red or blue food coloring in water. One person sprays color in snow every 10–20 feet, leading to a "treasure." You might try to confuse the treasure "seeker" by running around in the snow, creating false trails of footsteps.

INDEX

acid, test for, 91–92
airplanes. *see* planes
apron, 170–171

backpack, mini-, 118
backwards boy or girl costume, 157
backyard exercise course, 194
backyard orienteering treasure hunt, 201
backyard scavenger hunts, 196
balloon barometer, 78
balloons, helium, sending messages with, 192
barometer, balloon, 78
base, test for, 91–92
basket, paper, 44–45
beading crafts, 126–130
belt for costumes, 174
belt pack, 120
bird feeders, 177–180
board games
    costume, 167

homemade, 142–143
boats
    paper, 42–43
    walnut, 24
bookcase, instant, 25
bookmarks
    graphic, 54–55
    nature, 185
bubble bouncers, 86–87
bubble lettering, 56
bubbler, 191

candle and funnel, 77
candy machine costume, 159–160
cape, 170–171
caption drawings, 58
cardboard box bookcase, 25
cardboard box costumes, 159–164
cardboard box pet house, 25
cardboard tube rocket, 14
carnations, tissue, 30

castle, styrofoam tray, 16
caterpillar, egg-carton, 18–19
cereal box letter holder, 28
changing colors, 84–85
circles from straight lines, 98
clay, 63–71
clue to clue treasure hunt,
    202
codes, 144
colder snow, 88–89
collections, 136–139
colonial shoe buckles, 172
colonist costume, 158
colors
    changing, 84–85
    optical illusions with, 99, 100
comic strip, 59
cootie catcher, 48
cornstarch clay, 63–64
costumes, 152–158
    accessories for, 168–174
    cardboard box, 159–164
    sandwich board, 165–167
crayon crafts with fabric, 122–
    125
creature count, 193
cup, paper, 46
cutouts, drawing, 52

dalmatian costume, 155
dinner table costume, 161
doll house, 25
dolls
    backpack for, 118
    yarn, 104
dot lettering, 56
dough heads, 70–71
drawings
    caption, 58
    comic strip, 59
    cutouts, 52
    sidewalk, 189

earrings, costume, 174
egg-carton caterpillar, 18–19
egg-carton flowers, 22
ESP game, 141
exercise course, backyard, 194

fabric
    crayon crafts, 122–125
    sewing crafts, 107–120
fancy lettering, 56
five-point stars, 50
flashlight walk, 197
flowers
    bead necklace, 127–129
    cornstarch clay, 66–67
    costume, 156–157
    egg-carton, 22
    paper, 50
    tissue carnations, 30
    window garden, 32
flutter wing, 75
flying saucer, paper plate, 8–10
follow the arrows treasure hunt,
    199
follow the string treasure hunt,
    199–200
fortune teller, 48
funnel and candle, 77

games
    ESP, 141
    paper airplane, 42
    sidewalk, 188
    see also board games
George Washington costume,
    158
    wig for, 173
gift box costume, 164
gloves for costumes, 174
graphic bookmark, 54–55
gypsy/fortune teller costume, 153
    accessories for, 174

heads, dough, 70–71
helicopter, paper plate, 40–41
helium balloon message, 192
hippie costume, 154
hotter sunbeams, 79–80

Indian bead necklace, 129–130

juice box costume, 162

kerchief, 174
knickers, 173

letter holder, 28
lettering, 56–57
loops, paper, 82
lumberjack costume, 157

M & M costume, 166
magazines, writing to, 148
maps, 145–146
    treasure hunt, 202
masks, keeping on, 169
mice, walnut, 23
milk carton bird feeder, 180
mini-backpack, 118
mobile, 65–66
Möbius strip, 80–81
movable masterpiece costume,
    166
mummy costume, 154
mural, 3-D, 7–8

nature bookmark, 185
nature prints, 183–185
necklaces
    bead, 126–130, 168
    pouch, 117
neighborhood hunt, 202
newspaper, write your own,
    148–149
note cards, 60–61

optical illusions, 93–100

paint, stenciling with, 61–62
paper basket, 44–45
paper boat, 42
paper crafts, 37–62
paper cup, 46
paper loops, 82
paper plane, 37–38
paper plate flying saucer, 8–10
paper plate helicopter, 40–41
paper plate plane, 39
paper plate sunburst hanging,
    53
papier-mâché crafts, 34–36
Paul Bunyan costume, 157
pencil riders, 4
penny cleaner, 87
pepper/powder trick, 83–84
pet house, 25
pillows
    crayon craft, 124
    shape, 110
    tooth, 108–109
pine cone bird feeder, 177
pipe cleaner people, 4
pirate costume, 154
    accessories for, 174
placemats, 187
planes
    games with, 42
    paper, 37–38
    paper plate, 39
pocket bubbler, 191
politician costume, 158
pom-poms, 106
poster, 135
pot holder, 124–125
potpourri, 191
pouch, 115–117
powder/pepper trick, 83–84
purple cabbage water, 90–91

racing spiders, 20–21
rock star costume, 153
rockets
  cardboard tube, 14
  trolley, 10–12
rolling tubes, 76

sachets, 111
sandwich board costumes, 165–167
scavenger hunts, 196
scrapbook, 134
season placemats, 187
sew-a-picture, 103
sewing crafts, 107–120
shape pillow, 110
shoe buckles, colonial, 172
sidewalk games, 188–189
silver bead necklace, 168
snow
  colder, 88–89
  sculpture in, 197
  treasure hunt in, 202
soda bottle bird feeder, 178
song writing, 150
spiders, racing, 20–21
spinner, optical, 93–94
spirals, tunnels from, 97
sponge prints, 182
square piece of paper, how to
  make, 44
star gazing, 198
starch, test for, 89
stars, paper, 50
stenciling with paint, 61–62
stitches, basic, 107–108
straight lines, circles from, 98
stuffed animals
  backpack for, 118
  easy, 112–114

house for, 25
styrofoam tray castle, 16
sunbeams, hotter, 79–80
sunburst hanging, 53–54
superhero costume, 153

television set costume, 163–164
theme lettering, 56
3-D lettering, 56
3-D mural, 7–8
time capsule, 133–134
tissue carnations, 30
tooth pillow, 108–109
toothpick structures, 68
treasure hunts, 199–202
trolley rocket, 10–12
tube of toothpaste costume,
  165
tunnels from spirals, 97
twin, instant, 3
twirler, optical, 94–96

vitamin C, test for, 90

wallhanging, 123
walnut boats, 24
walnut mice, 23
wig for George Washington costume, 173
window garden, 32
word searches, 140
writing
  to magazines, 148
  newspaper, 148–149
  songs, 150

X marks the spot treasure hunt,
  200

yarn crafts, 103–106